THE STORY OF WINCHESTER

THE STORY
OF
WINCHESTER

Norman Wymer

STAPLES PRESS LIMITED
LONDON

FIRST PUBLISHED 1955
Copyright Reserved
This Book is set in the 'Monotype' Baskerville series

Made and printed in England by
STAPLES PRINTERS LIMITED
at their Rochester, Kent, establishment

CONTENTS

ILLUSTRATIONS

7

Illustrations

AUTHOR'S NOTE

THIS book is not intended to be an exhaustive history; nor is it a complete guide. Rather is it a kind of summary of the best of Winchester as seen through the eyes of just one of the thousands of pilgrims who still visit the ancient capital each year.

In the hope that such a method will prove of benefit to others who visit Winchester, as well as to the citizens themselves, I have married the historical to the guide book, summarizing the history of the town, the cathedral, the College and St Cross in general style in certain of the chapters, and analysing in greater detail various points of interest in others. In the case of the cathedral, for instance, I have devoted one chapter to its history, another to its bishops and the parts they have played, and a third to the various material features to be seen today. This third chapter I have produced in tabulated form, showing what to look for in each section of the building, in the hope that this will provide easy reference during an actual visit to the cathedral. I have followed the same principle when writing of the College.

For a great deal of the information regarding the College I have to thank Mr John Harvey, Consultant Architect and Archivist to Winchester College; and I wish to thank the Warden and Fellows for kindly allowing me to take the photographs of the school contained in this book.

NORMAN WYMER

Chapter One

A BRIEF HISTORY OF WINCHESTER

LONG centuries before Christianity came to England the
story of Winchester began; long before the birth of Christ
folk dwelt here in primitive homes comprising mere hollows
in the ground which they excavated by means of home-made
flint implements and the shoulder blades of oxen and then
roofed with a framework of tree branches, roughly thatched
with turfs, bracken, or anything else that happened to be
handy.

The canvas is too torn and faded to give us a clear picture
of Winchester's earliest days, but here and there odd features
still stand out to reveal a few facets. Evidence of an early
Iron Age trench by St Catherine's Hill – one of Winchester's
most famous landmarks, familiar to Wykehamists as 'Hills' –
gives reason to suppose, for instance, that this hill served as
a Celtic stronghold as far back as the third century B.C. Possibly its position near the navigable River Itchen caused the
Celts to regard the site as ideal for a market centre, while the
fact that there was an eminence from which to look down
upon attackers gave the place a certain natural security that
was very valuable in such times.

Somewhere about 50 B.C. it seems that the Itchen was used
for less peaceful purposes than the mere transport of produce.
For, in that year or thereabouts a band of Belgic invaders
sailed up the river to burn the gates of that old Celtic stronghold, driving out the occupants and establishing a new centre
under the name of Venta Belgarum.

But if the earliest picture has faded that of life under the
Romans is still reasonably clear in parts. About the middle of

the first century A.D. the Romans, under their emperor, Claudius, landed on the Hampshire coast – probably at a spot near Southampton – and proceeded to sail up the Itchen through the dense southern forests to the point in the river valley where Winchester now stands. Here they built one of their many camps and established a capital under the single name of Venta. True to their usual policy, they surrounded this town with a protective wall containing four main gates. Each of these gates faced one of the four points of the compass; and from these they laid down five important roads. From West Gate a road ran to Old Sarum by Salisbury; from East Gate another led to Portchester; the southern route pointed to what is now Southampton; while from Northgate two roads led respectively to Cirencester and Silchester, the last one of the most important of all Roman towns.

Within the walls of this Roman capital two main streets – one running from north to south and the other from east to west – crossed one another at right angles in the form of a cross, thus dividing the city into four distinct, though not equal, sections. In the south-western, where the castle hall now stands, the Romans set up their Law Courts; in the south-eastern, upon the site of the cathedral and its close, they erected their temples to their gods and sank their healing wells.

How the Romans passed their days in their stronghold of Venta no one can say, but, since many coins of both Nero and Claudius have been excavated here from time to time, it would seem that they suffered from no shortage of money. Besides marketing their farm produce, they were doubtless quick to establish various manufacturing trades and crafts; and, according to an old Roman document, they had developed, by the fourth century, an important and flourishing weaving centre where they carded, spun and wove the wool of the local downland sheep.

In the early years of the fifth century the Romans departed again – as suddenly, and probably as dramatically, as they had arrived in the first place. With their departure the story of Winchester turns several pages upon which is written, first a tale of gradual decay and neglect and then a more encouraging tale of the efforts of the Saxons to build up and consolidate their kingdom of Wessex.

By 519 Winchester is seen once more in glory. Like the Romans before them, the Saxons also valued this fortress by the Itchen; and in that year, so the Anglo-Saxon Chronicle tells us, they decided to make Winchester the capital of their kingdom of Wessex, appointing the 'Twain Aldermen', Cerdic and Cymric, as their rulers. Indeed, Winchester rose to such importance that the Hampshire capital is the only town, other than London, to find a place on an Anglo-Saxon map of the British Isles now housed in the archives of Hereford Cathedral.

Rather less than a hundred and twenty years on, and this now royal town also becomes an important centre of Christianity as the missionary bishop, St Birinus, sent by the Pope to convert the heathen Saxons, baptizes King Cynegils, and the latter, in gratitude, awards the saint, as we shall see later, measures of land at both Winchester and Dorchester (Oxon) for the building of churches.

The pages of our scrapbook now turn to the year 829, bringing Winchester still greater glory. Having defeated the Mercians and been accepted by the Northumbrians as their suzerain, King Egbert is universally acknowledged supreme ruler. At once the triumphant king gathers his courtiers and holds council in the castle on Winchester's main hill, when all agree that henceforth the small island which they had partitioned into so many little kingdoms shall be united under the single name of 'Angle-land'.

Thus Winchester becomes the capital not only of Wessex but of all England.

Alas, the lot of a capital has never been an easy one: less still in the days when the overlords thought of their homes only in terms of castles. In the centuries to follow Winchester was to provide the target for many a bitter attack. Towards the end of Egbert's reign the Danes invaded Wessex; and the Danes continued to attack Winchester, from time to time, long after England's first king had been buried in splendour in the capital's first church. Indeed, so fierce did their attacks become that King Alfred – a native of Winchester, who learnt many of his lessons at the hands of the great bishop, St Swithun – was driven from the town. Happily, however, this setback proved to be only temporary, for though he lost most of his army during his retreat, Alfred had soon built himself a fleet of ships; and with these he proceeded to sink the Danish vessels in the Solent. Before long he had returned to his capital where he ordered that his prisoners be hanged on the walls of his palace as an example to any other would-be invaders. . . . And there he was able to remain for the rest of his reign, holding his courts and planning many of his greatest works in this town by the Itchen without further undue disturbance.

If King Alfred saved Winchester from a military point of view during his lifetime, he was also responsible, after death, for advancing the town's importance as a religious centre by expressing a wish in his will that his son and successor, Edward the Elder, should found in that city a Benedictine nunnery, Nunnaminster, and a new religious house, the latter to be known as New Minster in order to distinguish it from the cathedral, which was then referred to as Old Minster.

Hardly had the New Minster been completed and the canons appointed than the canons grew restive. The ghost of the great king walked, they said, haunting the new buildings and terrifying them all out of their lives. For the sake of their founder's soul, they begged King Edward to translate the body of his father from Old Minster to 'New'. Later, in 1109, the founder of England's navy was disturbed for the second time when another generation of monks – who by then had replaced the canons – decided that the nearness of the two minsters to one another was a great inconvenience, and so deserted New Minster for a more distant building called Hyde Abbey, taking with them the bones of King Alfred.

Meanwhile the attacks on Winchester continued. In 927 it was defeat for the Danes at the hands of the courageous Saxon, Earl Guy of Warwick, who, it was reported, was sped to victory with the aid of a friendly crow. The fighting had been hard and bitter all day with so little to choose between the two opposing armies that, in the end, everything depended upon a single combat between the Earl and the Danish giant, Colebrand. What the result might have been had this contest proved a struggle between man and man no one can tell, for, as it was, fortune favoured the noble Guy in a most unexpected way. Just at the crucial moment, when a single blow might well have proved decisive either way, a crow, so the story runs, flew straight at the giant's face, temporarily unsighting him.

Victory; but not for ever. In 1001 Winchester once again heard the march of Danish feet; and in 1014 it was defeat for the Saxons, Ethelred the Unready being forced to flee to Normandy and thus leave the throne vacant for Canute to ascend the following year.

Once the tumult and the shouting had died away, however, Winchester soon found that life under a Dane was not really so very different from life under a Saxon: that Canute, as overlord, was no better nor no worse than the majority of his predecessors. If nothing else, he was more generous than many of them. To Old Minster, where he was later to be buried, he awarded 'three hides of land called Hille'; that is to say, St Catherine's Hill. To King Alfred's New Minster he presented a magnificent cross of silver and gold for the altar.

Probably Canute's generosity to the city was second only to that of Alfred himself.

Saxon or Dane on the throne, the daily round of monarch, monk and manual labourer continued much the same. In their palace the kings, each in due turn, held regular conference with their bishop, adjudged disputes, and heard the heralds sound the horn for their monthly 'mote' or 'moot'. Then, in the evening, the sound of music or noisy laughter might be heard coming from the palace as the monks sang to the king, or the Court jesters provided more frivolous entertainment. When not attending their services or employed at the palace the monks themselves would be busy writing and illuminating their books to build up their valuable chained library, each volume of which may well have been worth as much as a ship or a house. The more learned of the monks would spend much of their time teaching, but those skilled with their hands preferred to devote their energies to such crafts as silversmithing, producing splendid gold and silver pieces for their churches. Meanwhile the cottage folk toiled in the fields, probably quite indifferent as to the nationality of their sovereign.

Upon the death of Canute in 1035 Winchester found herself reduced in status. But not for long. For five years the Hampshire town reverted to being the mere capital of Wessex, governed by Canute's second son, Hardicanute, while the Danish king's elder son, Harold, reigned over all England from London. At the end of those years, however, Harold had joined his father. Whereupon Hardicanute ascended the throne, and Winchester regained her proud place in the life of the nation.

Proud, but no longer quite so supreme. By then London, with her great waterway the Thames, was rising both in commercial and royal favour. In 958 King Edgar had been proclaimed king at a spot by London's river since known as Kingston; and when Edward the Confessor succeeded his

half-brother, Hardicanute, in 1042 it was at Westminster
that he chose to be crowned for the first time. Though he
underwent a second coronation at Winchester after he had
been on the throne for about a year, he still preferred to
spend the greater part of his time in London. Harold, too,
was crowned at Westminster, and, as far as can be seen, he
never once so much as visited Winchester, either before or
after his accession, even though his uncle was abbot of New
Minster and it was from Bosham, just across the Sussex border, that he set sail for his ill-fated meeting with Duke
William. . . . But, of course, things might have been very
different had not his reign been cut so short by the Conquest.

At the Conquest Winchester stood loyal by the memory of
England's native king. However he might be received in
other parts, William the Conqueror was to be granted no
easy access into the Hampshire capital. Led by Harold's
uncle, the abbot, the monks of New Minster put chain
armour over their habits and turned out to resist the invaders
– but only, alas, to meet inevitable death and cause 20,000
acres of their valuable lands to be confiscated and the minster
deprived, for many years to come, of the right to an abbot.

Resistance was violent but short-lived: the memories of the
citizens equally short. Rather less than ninety years before
the Conquest a second cathedral had been built by Bishop
Aethelwold to replace the first, and in this William the Conqueror was crowned in splendour in 1068, having previously
been crowned, like Edward the Confessor before him, at
Westminster. And the people of Winchester were lining the
streets to cheer him on his way. Whether their cheers were
feigned or heartfelt, it was said that this second ceremony
was by far the finer of the two; finer perhaps than anything
Winchester had yet witnessed. Most of the leading noblemen,
Norman and Saxon, loyal and disloyal alike, were in attend-
ance, and the service in the cathedral was followed by a
magnificent banquet when the king's champion, his massive

17

armour a-glitter, rode into the great hall of the castle challenging any one present to deny the right of William to the title of King of England – a custom which, incidentally, thereafter continued to be maintained at the coronation of every sovereign down to that of William IV.

If William the Conqueror was ruthless in his treatment of New Minster, Winchester as a town benefited enormously, both in prestige and materially, under his rule. Unlike his immediate predecessors, Edward the Confessor and Harold, he found Winchester a far more suitable centre than London. As Duke of Normandy, he still owned great estates in France, and these demanded personal visits every now and again. What more convenient for this than Winchester with its old Roman road leading down to the Channel port of Southampton? Since he found that he could also govern his newly-won kingdom of England as well from Hampshire as from Westminster, he decided to make London and Winchester the country's joint capitals, but proceeded to spend more of his time at Winchester.

Not content with the place as he found it, he immediately embarked, with typical Norman thoroughness, upon a vast new building programme such as would make it a capital really worthy of the name. Hardly had the streets been cleared of the arms and banners that greeted his coronation than teams of masons were at work in the four corners of the city. A proud conqueror must needs have a proud palace. Thus, before anything, a majestic home had to be erected for his benefit upon the site by the Square where now stands the little church of St Laurence. Here William set up his seat of government and established a treasury, complete with mints and standards of weights and measures. Before long the castle, too – the castle from which the Saxons had resisted the Danes – was being rebuilt. And before it was yet quite a century old work had begun on replacing Winchester's second cathedral with a third. Under this new programme many buildings of small but fine Saxon craftsmanship were swept away in favour of far mightier buildings whose very size spelt power.

Fortunately for Winchester, William was not merely the proud and vain conqueror which all this apparent opulence might have led the inhabitants to suppose him to be. Ambitious in his building programme, he was no less thorough in his method of administration. By careful planning he was able to bring prosperity to the town such as it had never enjoyed before; consequently many of the meaner folk, who hitherto had been unable to make ends meet, no longer lived in quite such poverty, while some of the more well-to-do citizens were able to amass quite comfortable fortunes.

A few years after his accession to the throne the Conqueror's son, William Rufus, added still further to the riches of the city by granting a charter for holding an annual fair on St Giles' Hill. The fair opened every year on the Eve of St Giles (August 31st) and lasted for three days until, in 1349, Edward III granted a further charter extending the period to sixteen days. The proceedings were in the charge of the bishop, who appointed his own mayor and bailiffs for the occasion, and then conducted his Pavilion Court of Justice within a palisaded enclosure. When the stage was set and ready the keys of the city were handed over to the bishop's officers and all normal trading in Winchester and Southampton and for seven leagues around the capital was brought to a compulsory standstill. Whereupon the air of Winchester hummed with the strange tongues of many countries as the merchants of Europe and the East mingled with the Hampshire folk, offering their carpets, wines and other wares in exchange for English wool and English hides.

If Winchester prospered through St Giles' Fair, her people had no other reason to feel grateful to the hard-hearted Rufus, whose reign in the town otherwise only caused them to appreciate the more the virtues of the Conqueror and

mourn the latter's passing. Nor did their troubles end with
the fatal hunting accident that saw their detested monarch
drawn back to the city on a farm cart for burial. A few years
of peace and quiet, and the pages of our scrapbook turn to
the reign of Stephen . . . and more trouble.

With the haughty Matilda, daughter of Henry I, strug-
gling desperately to seize the throne of England and the
turncoat Stephen striving as desperately to defend it, Winchester soon found herself a sorely tested centre of strife and
civil war with the fortunes of the two claimants alternately
ebbing and flowing. At one moment the Empress Matilda
holds the initiative by seizing the castle and proceeding to
bombard the capital, causing grievous damage to such
buildings as Nunnaminster and Hyde Abbey and the final
destruction of the Conqueror's palace, already damaged by
fire in 1103. At the next, Stephen proves triumphant; and the
inhabitants of Winchester watch a seemingly sad body of
men carry away their would-be queen in a leaden coffin –
not in death, as they supposed at the time, but as the first
phase of a humiliating retreat.

Before many more years had passed those who witnessed
that 'funeral' procession were acknowledging Matilda's son
as King Henry II. . . . And in 1184 Henry II advanced the
status of Winchester by granting her a Charter of Incorpora-
tion.

Yet though Henry thus raised the official standing of the
town and did all in his power to make good the harm
wrought by his mother and Stephen between them, Winchester's place as a royal capital was once more in jeopardy.
For Henry also showed undoubted preference for London.
So too did the Crusader king, Richard I, after him. Once
his coronation in the cathedral was over Richard was seen
no more in Winchester, though admittedly his constant
journeyings abroad to fight the Holy Wars left him but little
time in which to visit either town.

Under Henry III Winchester recovered her position for a time. Having been born in the city and christened in the cathedral's fine black font, this king had a native affection for the place which he was never to lose. Though unhappily he quarrelled with the monks, by the citizens as a whole he was loved as a kindly squire: so much so that whenever he returned to the city from London or elsewhere curtains and carpets were hung from the buildings and loyal banners displayed to greet him.

After the town had been sacked during the Baronial Wars of 1265 Edward I provided a further fillip by holding his first Parliament at Winchester in 1276, basing this upon Earl Simon de Montfort's 'House of Commons'. Another half-century or so, and the third Edward has appointed Winchester the principle wool mart of England, capping this honour a few years later, as I have already mentioned, by granting a further charter extending St Giles' Fair to sixteen days, a move designed largely to help the wool sales. Alas, Winchester was not to enjoy her newly-won position for long. Within thirty years she had lost her port for export to the Continent through the destruction of Southampton by the French and had suffered so sadly through the Black Death that the king deemed it wise to transfer the staple to Calais.

As the kings gradually turned more and more to London the power of the bishops increased. They often held the high office of Chancellor of the Realm, and upon the institution of the Order of the Garter the Bishop of Winchester was appointed, by virtue of his position, prelate of that noble order. Within the city itself they were granted complete jurisdiction, with practically vice-regal powers, over a wide area known as the Soke, so called from the Saxon 'soc', meaning liberty. This area included the cathedral precincts, the college, the Hospital of St Cross, and a large measure of land to the south of the town. Cheyney Court provided the bishop's seat of government, and here regular courts were conducted when twelve well-respected citizens would be summoned to serve as a jury. The courts were in the charge of a resident bailiff and a team of officials who, after each sitting, reported their findings to the bishop and recommended the punishments to be imposed on the miscreants. Such courts continued to hold session until two years before the accession of Queen Victoria when the municipal government of the town was reformed and the power of the bishops curtailed.

All through the Middle Ages, as we shall see later, the cathedral itself gradually became larger and more splendid as successive bishops added their own contributions to the fabric. As bishop and church alike advanced in stature so the see of Winchester gradually became the richest in the land, its wealth being enhanced to no small degree by the vast concourse of pilgrims who came annually to the cathedral to worship at the shrine of the beloved St Swithun, to whom the latest cathedral was dedicated. Thus whatever prestige Winchester may have lost as joint capital of England during those sadly disturbed, ever-changing, Middle Ages she gained as a religious centre.

Before the fourteenth century ended she had also become an educational centre whose importance was to increase with the centuries beyond the wildest expectations of those who saw it come into being. In 1382, while the town was still suffering from the aftermath of the Black Death and the resultant loss of the wool staple, one of the greatest of all Winchester's bishops, William of Wykeham, twice Chancellor of the Realm, founded the scholastic establishment of St Mary Winton which, as Winchester College, was to provide the seed-bed of the Public School system and the model for many similar foundations of the future.

Thereafter the story of Winchester is focused mainly upon the cathedral and the college. Nevertheless the royal links have not yet been wholly severed; the trumpets and the fanfares may still be heard from time to time from the castle on the hill. As we continue to turn the pages we still find many mentions of kings and queens and princes, and of their parliaments holding session in the ancient capital.

In 1386, just a year before William of Wykeham laid the foundation stones of the first buildings of his new college, the cathedral once more affords a scene of splendour as the guests arrive for the marriage of Henry Bolingbroke (later Henry IV) to the rich heiress, Mary de Bohun. Another thirty years, or rather less, and the splendour shifts to the castle, when Cardinal Beaufort entertains Henry V in style to wish him well as he prepares to set sail with his army to fight the Battle of Agincourt. In 1440 it is the turn of the college itself to decorate its buildings – or such as are completed – as Henry VI pays a visit to the school in order to study conditions with a view to founding a similar establishment at Eton.

Then, in 1486, comes a royal birth: the birth at Winchester of Henry VII's eldest son, Prince Arthur, followed by his christening in the cathedral. And after that the celebration of victory when the second Tudor, Henry VIII, recently returned from his triumphs at the Field of the Cloth of Gold, receives the emperor, Charles V, at the castle in the year of 1522. . . . Victory for England but, alas, soon to be followed by a sad moment for Winchester when Henry's Chancellor, Cardinal Wolsey, decides to dissolve the monasteries, and all of the city's religious houses with the exception of the cathedral are obliged to surrender their treasures and close their doors.

For a time all is now gloom until, in 1554, the scene is once again brightened temporarily by the brilliant spectacle of a royal wedding. Now it is for the marriage of Queen Mary to Philip of Spain that the hundreds of candles in the cathedral are lit and the highly colourful cavalcade of troops lines the streets. Only at a coronation had Winchester witnessed a

23

more dazzling display than this. Yet within little more than twelve months Mary was a wife without a husband; and in just over four years she was dead.

The Queen is dead, long live the Queen. . . . Sixteen years after that wedding the people of Winchester were hovering about the streets hoping to catch a glimpse of Mary's sister, Elizabeth I, as she too came to visit the college.

The bright and glorious Elizabethan age closes, and a new one opens with the Union of England and Scotland under James I. Conditions in London in that year of 1603, the year of accession, were hardly auspicious; hardly inviting to a man accustomed to the fresh and healthy breezes of the north. For the dreaded plague was taking terrible toll of life in London. Since James had no desire to be numbered among its victims, one of his first acts upon ascending the throne was to move with his courtiers to the comparative safety of Winchester and thither to transfer his Law Courts, requisitioning the buildings of Wykeham's college in order to accommodate the judges and serjeants and other officials.

Another dark hour had struck. The Scottish king had no love for Elizabethan favourites, least of all for that gallant adventurer who had once laid his cloak in the path of his queen and had sailed the high seas time and again trying to annex new territories to her empire. When it came to his ears through the lips of those involved in the many intrigues that characterized the close of Elizabeth's court that Sir Walter Raleigh was planning to place his (the king's) cousin, Arabella Stuart, on the throne in his stead, James, without seeking further confirmation, stripped Raleigh of his possessions and ordered the latter's immediate arrest. Thus one of the first to be tried at the Winchester courts was Sir Walter himself. . . . And Winchester was soon to learn the shallowness of British justice in that unhappy seventeenth century. As history records, the trial was a farce from beginning to end with the conclusion reached before the proceedings opened. Though Raleigh made a spirited and convincing defence and thus regained the popularity of the populace, he was condemned to death and sent to the Tower.

The trial of Raleigh, hideous in itself, was but a sad portent of still worse things to come: a curtain raiser to a long period of stress for Winchester. The Civil War and the plague each had a niche to carve in the history of Winchester, and Judge Jeffreys was to hold his well-named 'Bloody Assize' in the town before the seventeenth century was out.

As might be expected of a town so firmly linked with the monarchy, Winchester was staunchly Royalist at the outbreak of the Civil War. . . . Loyal at heart but, alas, too weak at arms. After a siege of but six days the Cromwellians, under their general, Sir William Waller, stormed the gates in 1642 to plunder and pillage. Having sacked buildings right and left and seized all the treasures that appeared worthwhile, they seem to have been content to let matters stand for the moment. For within a matter of months the victorious soldiery had mostly departed again, leaving virtually no garrison behind them – and the stage clear for the return of the Royalists. Soon Lord Ogle, supported by the famous general, Lord Hopton, was in command of the city, and the people of Winchester were busily raising £30,000 to help fight the cause of Charles I. Winchester, however, was not to remain in peace for long. In the villages round about, Royalists and Cromwellians alike were building up their forces for that great last battle which must decide every military issue. . . . And in 1644, the year before the Royalist cause suffered its final eclipse at Naseby, that battle was fought on Cheriton Down, not far from the little village of that name, when Waller's forces routed those of Hopton and the other generals and so cleared the way for their final capture of Winchester, close on 2,500 men perishing in the struggle.

For sixteen years the people of Winchester now had to bow to their new Puritan masters, watching the castle of their kings slighted and many of their loveliest buildings damaged beyond repair, powerless to do anything but implore their conquerors to at least spare their cathedral: a request that was reluctantly granted, but only after that building had been seriously despoiled and most of the buildings in the close wrecked.

Sixteen long years of neglect and destruction – and then the ignominious retreat of those who had caused such havoc. No town, surely, can have felt more jubilant over the Restoration than Winchester; and in 1665 those first feelings of relief gave way to feelings of triumph as she welcomed, once more, a king to her midst. Like James I before him, Charles II also decided to set up his headquarters in Winchester in order to avoid the plague in London. Scarcely had the king arrived, however, than a further cloud cast dark shadows over the scene so recently brightened. The plague of 1665, unhappily, proved to be far more virulent than the plague of 1603; and far more widespread. Soon the dreaded purple spots had appeared in Winchester too, wiping out whole families within a matter of days. The gates of the city had to be closed, barring all entrance and exit, while for weeks on end the citizens of Winchester were obliged to live upon the charity of the country folk round about, who would trudge, several times a week, on foot or horseback, from the surrounding villages bringing fresh produce. This they would place on a stone by West Gate; whereupon, in return, the grateful inhabitants dropped coins into a trough of vinegar by way of payment for their saviours to collect upon their next visit. Meanwhile, within the city itself, the unhappy sufferers buried their dead in communal graves almost daily.

So virulent was the epidemic that the king was obliged to leave Winchester almost as soon as he arrived. But when the city was free of infection he was back again; and he grew so deeply attached to the place that in 1682 he decided to commission none other than the great Sir Christopher Wren himself to build him a new palace in the city. It was to be a splendid palace, finer by far than even that of Versailles, and before the year had ended Sir Christopher was already at work on the new venture and had become a familiar figure in the streets.

Was Winchester, after all these years of trouble, to become once more a great capital of England? her people asked. Such, indeed, appears to have been the king's intention; such might well have been, had not fate once again played a part. Before Sir Christopher's fine new creation was even nearing completion Charles II was dead; and Winchester had sung her swan-song as a royal capital.

Chapter Two

A CALENDAR OF WINCHESTER EVENTS

B.C.

St Catherine's Hill, one of Winchester's best known landmarks, believed to have served as a primitive stronghold and market place at least since the third century B.C.

c. 50   St Catherine's Hill stormed by Belgic invaders who burn the gates, drive out the occupants, and establish a new centre under the name of Venta Belgarum where Winchester now stands.

A.D.

c. 43   The Romans, under Claudius, arrive to build the walled town and fort of Venta with five main roads leading to Old Sarum, Portchester, Southampton, Cirencester and Silchester.

During their occupation the Romans establish an important weaving factory for the preparation and manufacture of wool from the local downland sheep.

c. 410   The Romans abandon Winchester.

519   The Roman market town and fort of Venta becomes the capital of the newly-founded Saxon kingdom of Wessex, ruled over by the 'Twain Aldermen', Cerdic and Cymric.

534   The death of Cerdic and burial at Winchester.

635   The missionary bishop, Birinus, is sent to England by the Pope to convert the Saxons. He converts the Saxon king, Cynegils, establishes a new bishopstool at Dorchester in Oxfordshire and builds a church at

The West Front of Winchester Cathedral as rebuilt by Bishop Edington.

The Deanery, Winchester.

Winchester Cathedral from the south-west, showing the single tower.

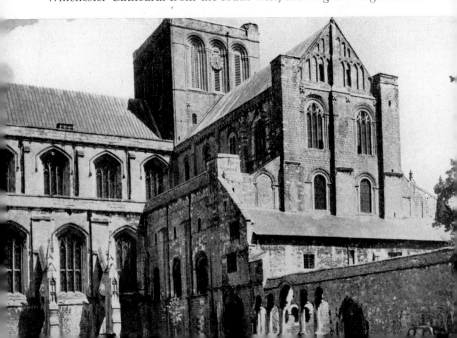

Winchester on land given to him in gratitude by Cynegils.

643   Death of Cynegils.

648   Winchester's church is dedicated to Saints Peter and Paul on Christmas Day at a ceremony of great splendour.

676   The seat of the Wessex bishopric, together with the bones of Birinus, is transferred from Dorchester to Winchester by the missionary's son, Bishop Haeddi.

802   Egbert ascends the throne at Winchester.

829   Having defeated the Mercians and been accepted by the Northumbrians as their suzerain, Egbert becomes the first king of all 'Angle-land'. As a result, Winchester becomes the capital not only of Wessex but of England.

836   Death of King Egbert and burial at Winchester.

852   St Swithun is appointed Bishop of Winchester.

858   King Aethelwulf, father of King Alfred, is buried at Winchester.

860   Winchester is seriously damaged by fire in the first of a series of raids which are conducted by the Danes during the second half of this century.

862   Death of St Swithun and burial in the cathedral churchyard.

871   King Alfred, who was privately tutored in the Hampshire capital by St Swithun, ascends the throne at Winchester.

c. 901   Death of King Alfred and burial at Winchester, and the accession of his son, Edward the Elder.

c. 901   A new monastic establishment to be known as New Minster, together with a Benedictine nunnery, Nunnaminster, are set up by Edward the Elder in accordance with a wish expressed in his father's will.

c. 903   Alfred's bones are translated to New Minster at the request of the monks.

927   Invading Danes defeated by Guy of Warwick who, according to local legend, was aided in his conquest by a friendly crow.

955   Death of King Edred and burial at Winchester.

959   Edgar ascends the throne at Winchester.

971   The bones of St Swithun are translated from the churchyard to the new cathedral now being constructed to replace the church erected by Birinus. Upon the start of the translation the rains descend for forty days and nights, thus giving rise to the current legend concerning St Swithun's Day.

975   Death and burial at Winchester of King Edgar.

978   Ethelred the Unready ascends the throne at Winchester at the age of ten.

980   Winchester's second cathedral (known as Old Minster) is completed by Bishop Aethelwold and dedicated to St Swithun. Upon the orders of St Dunstan, Archbishop of Canterbury, the canons are replaced by Benedictine monks.

1014   Ethelred the Unready is defeated by the Danes and forced to flee to Normandy, thus making way for Canute to ascend the throne at Winchester the following year.

1035   Death of Canute and burial in Winchester's new cathedral. Wessex once again becomes, temporarily, a separate kingdom with Canute's eldest son king of England and Hardicanute ruler of Wessex.

1040   Upon the death of Canute's eldest son Hardicanute becomes king of all England.

1042   Death of Hardicanute and burial at Winchester.

1043   Edward the Confessor is crowned in Winchester Cathedral, having already been crowned at Westminster.

1066   William the Conqueror makes Winchester his joint capital of England with London, finding the Hampshire town a convenient centre from which to pay periodic visits to his estates in Normandy.

1068 William the Conqueror, already crowned at Westminster, is crowned for the second time at Winchester; and here builds himself a palace.

1079 Bishop Walkelin, kinsman of the Conqueror, begins work on the building of the present cathedral, Winchester's third.

1093 The new cathedral is consecrated before a rich assembly of bishops, abbots and statesmen.

1093 The bones of St Swithun are disturbed for the second time to be translated to the new cathedral. There the saint's shrine becomes the object of great and glorious pilgrimages.

c.1094 A chapel is established on St Catherine's Hill in honour of St Catherine, a martyred virgin saint, to be replaced later by a larger chapel and priest's house. In later years this chapelry was suppressed by Cardinal Wolsey.

1096 William Rufus grants a charter for holding a three-days' fair at the hill of St Giles, to begin on the Eve of St Giles (August 31st).

1100 William Rufus, killed by an arrow in the New Forest while hunting, is buried in Winchester Cathedral.

1103 William the Conqueror's palace is seriously damaged by fire.

1109 The monks desert New Minster for a new building, Hyde Abbey, taking with them the bones of King Alfred.

1136 The Hospital of St Cross, believed to be the oldest almshouse in the kingdom, is founded by Bishop Henry de Blois, half-brother of King Stephen.

c.1140 The Empress Matilda seizes Winchester Castle and from there bombards the capital, causing much destruction.

1184	The city is granted its Charter of Incorporation by Henry II.
1195	Richard I, the Crusader King, is crowned in Winchester Cathedral for the second time.
1207	Henry III is born at Winchester.
1213	King John is reconciled to Archbishop Stephen Langton at Winchester.
1265	Winchester is sacked during the Baronial wars.
1276	Edward I holds his first Parliament at Winchester, basing this upon Simon de Montfort's 'House of Commons'.
1289	The Hospital of St John is founded.
c.1333	Winchester is appointed Chief Woolmart of England by Edward III but loses the staple to Calais thirty years later.
1349	Edward III grants the city a further charter extending St Giles' Fair to sixteen days.
1382	William of Wykeham, Bishop of Winchester and a former pupil of the city's Grammar School, founds Winchester College, and thus establishes the Public School system.
1386	Henry IV is married in Winchester Cathedral.
1387	The first stones of the new college are laid.
1394	The buildings of Wykeham's new college of Winton are occupied for the first time.
1404	Death of William of Wykeham and burial in Winchester Cathedral in a chantry of his own design.
1415	Henry V is entertained by Cardinal Beaufort in Winchester Castle before setting sail to fight the Battle of Agincourt.
1440	Henry VI visits Winchester College to study conditions there prior to founding Eton College.
1486	Prince Arthur, eldest son of Henry VII, is born at Winchester and christened in the cathedral.
1522	The Emperor Charles V visits Henry VIII at Win-

chester Castle after the latter's return from the Field of the Cloth of Gold.

*c.*1538   Hyde Abbey, by then one of the wealthiest of the smaller religious houses in the south and the burial place of King Alfred and other Saxon kings and saints, is dissolved by Henry VIII and pillaged, together with St Swithun's Priory and St Elizabeth's College.

1554   Mary Tudor and Philip of Spain, having both stayed the previous nights in the city, are married in Winchester Cathedral at a ceremony of great splendour.

1570   Queen Elizabeth visits Winchester College.

1603   Because of the plague in London the Law Courts are moved by James I to Winchester Castle and the college is requisitioned to accommodate the judges and serjeants.

1603   At these courts Sir Walter Raleigh is tried on a trumped-up charge of plotting against the king, sentenced to death and given temporary reprieve.

1642   Winchester, Royalist by heart and tradition, is captured by the Cromwellians under Sir William Waller after a siege of only six days.

1644   The Royalists suffer final defeat at the Battle of Cheriton Down, near Winchester.

1648   Charles I passes through the city on the way to his trial.

1665   Charles II moves the Court to Winchester to avoid the plague in London.

1666   The plague spreads to Winchester and takes heavy toll of the inhabitants.

1682   Charles II commissions Sir Christopher Wren to build a new royal palace at Winchester; a work that was never completed.

1685   Judge Jeffreys holds 'Bloody Assize' in the Castle

Hall at Winchester. At these trials he sentenced the elderly Lady Alice Lisle to death for harbouring one of Monmouth's soldiers and ordered her to be beheaded in the Square.

1762   The clump of trees on St Catherine's Hill, a famous landmark, is planted by the militia to mark the site of St Catherine's chapelry.

1770   The citizens of Winchester turn out to guard the city cross and prevent its removal when it is sold to a private landowner for use in his grounds.

1901   The millenary of Alfred the Great is celebrated in the city, and a statue is erected to his memory.

1905   A seven-year task of underpinning the cathedral at a cost of £113,000 is begun.

1912   A thanksgiving service for the preservation of the cathedral through so many centuries is held on St Swithun's Day, attracting a large number of pilgrims headed by King George V.

Chapter Three

THE CATHEDRAL STORY

ON the low-lying land where Winchester Cathedral now stands – a land once no better than a spongy morass, riddled with fresh-water springs which proved a constant source of magic and wonderment to those who beheld them – little tribes of Belgic folk encamped, performed their pagan fertility rites, lit their funeral pyres, buried the ashes of their dead, close on 2000 years ago.

Here the Romans, following after, sank their healing wells and erected temples to their vain and strange gods – to Jupiter and Nero and Minerva, and no doubt to many others.

The Romans departed; the Saxons arrived. The Saxons were less orderly than the well-regimented Romans: by comparison they proved uncouth and, at times, perhaps even barbarous. Yet, like those before them, they too worshipped their gods – Thor and Odin now – cast pins or coins into the waters of the wells in the hope of bringing themselves luck, and buried their dead on the marshes by the Itchen.

Belgics, Romans, Saxons followed one another at their heathen worship with no thought for any other site. But then, in 634, Saint Birinus landed on the Hampshire coast, having been sent to England by the Pope, charged with the unpromising task of roaming around the countryside converting as many as possible of the seemingly irresponsible Saxon chieftains.

Among the first of his converts was Cynegils, king of the Wessex kingdom, whom he baptized the year after his arrival. As is so often the case with converts of any kind,

35

Cynegils became devout, and an enthusiastic follower of Birinus. To the saint he granted measures of land at both Winchester and Dorchester in Oxfordshire upon which to build churches. The Winchester grant included not only the marshland by the River Itchen but also a strip of country extending for some seven miles around the town which the king intended should provide the revenues for the support of the church.

Upon his land at Dorchester Birinus at once proceeded to erect an abbey as a house of secular canons, and this he used as his bishopstool; while at Winchester he built a second church which, though then naturally of lesser importance, he dedicated on Christmas Day 648 to Saints Peter and Paul at a most colourful ceremony that was said to have attracted most of the leading figures in the realm.

In little more than a quarter of a century this second church had surpassed the first in importance. For in 676 the see was transferred from Dorchester to Winchester by Birinus's son, and the church on the marshes was promoted to the rank of cathedral. Thereafter, in the centuries to follow, Winchester gradually grew into one of the richest sees in the country – if not the richest – with its bishops enjoying high office in the State.

Of those who helped to enrich Winchester in her early days as a cathedral city probably none did more than St Swithun, a native of the town who taught King Alfred many of his lessons and who was created bishop in 852, a post which he held until his death ten years later. A simple, kindly man by nature, it was said that by his very example he caused the people to live virtuously and attend church regularly. He travelled for miles around his diocese on foot to visit the sick and the poor, and such was his generosity that if ever a church fell into disrepair he had the damage made good at his own expense.

In life he was respected and loved by people of all walks

and all classes. Yet it was in death that he brought the greatest material riches to his cathedral – and he brought them, ironically, in a way which he would have strongly condemned and which, even as one of his last dying commands, he did his best to guard against. Fearing that were he to be buried in a shrine within the church itself his followers might adopt the fashion of the times and pay pilgrimages to his tomb instead of coming to Winchester to worship God, St Swithun called together his canons and expressed a wish for a simple burial in the churchyard outside. That wish was granted.

Alas, the saint was not to be left for ever at peace in the spot of his own choosing. Within a few decades of his death the Danes had arrived to sack the simple structure set up by Birinus, and in the second half of the tenth century another bishop, Aethelwold, was superintending the building of a second and more elaborate cathedral together with a number of conventual buildings for Benedictine monks. The walls had risen to just about half of their intended height when the masons – or was it the canons? – noticed the ground around St Swithun's grave splitting open and, so it is said, 'the earth heaving as though the saint were pleading for reburial within the new edifice'. So convinced was everyone who witnessed this scene that this was a portent that on July 15th, 971, they decided to open the grave. . . . But lo, hardly had the first spade turned the first sod than the heavens began to weep. For forty days and forty nights it continued to rain as if in protest, creating such an impression upon those engaged in the translation that they declared that ever after a wet St Swithun's day would be followed by a further forty days of rain.

When at last the storms subsided and it was possible to continue with the saint's translation into the new cathedral Winchester became one of the most important pilgrimage centres in Europe. From the four corners they came – men, women and children of all classes and in all conditions to worship at the shrine of St Swithun, there to pray for better health or to give thanks for the cure of their ills and then, upon leaving, to make their silver offerings. For six hundred years, right down to the Reformation, they continued to come, this constant stream of pilgrims. And as their numbers multiplied, generation by generation, so the riches of Winchester increased.

By 980 this second cathedral was completed. Upon the instructions of St Dunstan, the great reforming Archbishop of Canterbury and patron saint of the blind, Bishop Aethelwold had by then replaced the canons by the Benedictine monks, thus making the new building a monastic church as well as a cathedral; and in that same year of 980 leading figures of both Church and State were again attending a ceremony of dedication as their forebears had done three centuries previously. This time the cathedral was dedicated not only to Saints Peter and Paul but to St Swithun as well.

This second church was probably as fine as any yet seen; and it was equipped, records a contemporary monk, with an organ no less magnificent – an enormous affair of 400 pipes and twenty-six bellows that were operated by 'seventy strong men, labouring with their arms, covered with perspiration, each inciting his companions to drive the wind up with all his strength'. The music of this tremendous instrument, the monk tells us, broke like thunder through the town of Winchester and across the hills beyond so that people in the streets were unable to hear themselves speak through the noise.

In this cathedral and to the music of this organ both Canute and Hardicanute were buried and Edward the Confessor and William the Conqueror were crowned. The church became the scene of pageantry as yet unrivalled. For the Normans, however, the church was nowhere near fine enough. Thus, almost exactly a hundred years after its completion, in 1079, another team of masons, tilers, paviours, glaziers and the rest were making their way to the marshes to embark upon the building of yet a third church – the mighty edifice we see today.

The new building was designed partly for the benefit of the monks who lived in the cloister, partly for the bishop of the diocese, and partly as a place in which to house the earthly remains of Winchester's saints and kings. Though Winchester had long served as the bishopstool it was not intended, at that stage, to provide a diocesan centre such as is known today; nor was it even anticipated that in time the church would acquire the status of a national monument, although one would have supposed that the number of pilgrims already visiting Winchester to do homage to St Swithun might have given at least a hint of things to come. The new church, therefore, had many purposes to serve but without any ecclesiastic need for undue grandeur.

A new era of church building had arrived with the Normans, however. Upon the orders of William the Conqueror cathedrals now had to be sited in towns rather than villages, as had been the case with the Saxons; while everywhere churches became larger and more magnificent – though not necessarily finer or more beautiful – than any built in Saxon times. As capital, home of kings and seat of parliaments, it was natural that Winchester should have the most magnificent cathedral of all, save possibly that of London, now ranked with Winchester as joint-capital of England.

So it was to be. The third cathedral, when completed, was second only to old St Paul's in size. The work was supervised by Winchester's first Norman bishop, one Walkelin, who, by all accounts, was a relative of William the Conqueror. Wiser than his Saxon predecessors, Walkelin worked upon the sensible theory that a city built upon poor foundations cannot stand, and so decided that before he gave thought to his walls he must lay a firm bed for them in those marshy bogs.

But a bed of what? Since there was no such thing as concrete in those days and since transport, other than by water,
had to be carried out by means of the pack-horse, he had to
make do with whatever reasonably suitable material was
nearest to hand in sufficient quantities. The best that
Walkelin could find was trees. There were many fine oaks
and beech trees in nearby Hempage Woods, and these the
bishop resolved to obtain. This, however, proved to be
easier said than done, for the owner of those trees was none
other than the king himself. Though William the Conqueror
was well enough disposed in the ordinary way towards his
kinsman, the bishop, he was far better disposed towards the
sport of hunting the stag. The trees afforded good cover for
the stag and the various other beasts of the chase, and he was
loath to see them go. Indeed, had the request been made by
anyone but a relative the king would no doubt have turned
it down out of hand; as it was, he agreed, rather grudgingly,
to allow his bishop the right to any timber he could remove
during the course of four days and nights.

If William had imagined his woods to be safeguarded by
so subtle an offer, if he assumed it impossible to remove more
than one or two trees in so brief a period, he was soon to be
sadly disillusioned. The permission to fell having once been
obtained, Bishop Walkelin summoned every man and boy
he could find and led them all into Hempage Woods. There
the saws and axes worked unceasingly until by the end of
the four days the woods had given place to a barren stretch
of stumps, the whole wide open to the sky. Only one tree
remained: a gnarled and elderly oak which the bishop had
taken care to preserve because local tradition had it that St
Augustine had once preached under its branches a few years
after his arrival in England with his forty black-robed monks.
These oaks and beeches – sturdy trees, all of them – Bishop
Walkelin laid side by side in the marshy, water-logged soil to
provide his 'foundation sure'.

Meanwhile boats were making their way up the Itchen in slow but steady procession bringing large quantities of stone from the Isle of Wight for the actual building. For fourteen years master masons and their teams of workmen and apprentices then carved and dressed those great slabs and laid them, skilfully and majestically, one upon the other, to form their noble arches.

By 1093 the enormous task was complete, and two cathedrals stood close to one another on the marshes – a mighty Norman cruciform church which successive monarchs throughout a great part of the Middle Ages were to attend every Easter, wearing their crowns, and which, as the years passed, was to grow mightier still; and a Saxon church, once all-important but now dwarfed, supplanted, and seemingly humble, and soon to disappear altogether. Being designed not only for the bishop of the diocese but also for the Benedictine monks, this third cathedral was divided into two sections by a screen or pulpitum a little to the west of the present choir. Upon this fine screen were displayed many treasures including King Canute's crown and a magnificent silver cross that had been presented to the old cathedral by Queen Emma, wife of Ethelred. While the monks were to hold their services to the east of this pulpitum, the public were to assemble for their worship to the west of it. With this idea in mind the stonework at the eastern end was left in its natural state but, at the western end, was elaborately decorated with murals and painted emblems and devices to provide the perfect setting for the religious festivals so popular in the Middle Ages when people were accustomed to attend in costly raiment and carrying colourful banners.

On the eighth day of April that year all the leading prelates and statesmen of the country congregated in Winchester for a third grand ceremony of dedication: the grandest of all. A few weeks later St Swithun was disturbed for the second time when his bones were removed from the old Saxon cathedral and placed in a shrine behind the high altar of the Norman; shortly afterwards the bones of St Birinus, the founder of the see, were likewise translated from Dorchester to Winchester, together with the remains of other saints and kings.

Some five years after that splendid consecration Bishop Walkelin himself died. He had prayed, it was said, to be spared 'further miseries of life' after William II had begun to dun him for £200 which he was unable to raise without robbing the poor; and his prayers had been answered. He was buried in his own cathedral with a splendour that was rendered the more heartfelt by the cause of his death. Before another two years had passed the detested William Rufus himself had been laid in his own cold grave under the central tower of that building, having been drawn back in the rudest fashion to Winchester from his unfortunate hunting 'accident' in the New Forest, arrow still in heart, upon a farm cart by a people who, far from displaying grief or respect, made no attempt to conceal their joy at the thought that they were seeing the last of a tyrant.

Alas, another accident was to attend the unpopular king even in his final sleep. Within less than a decade, in 1107, the whole tower above his tomb collapsed and crashed to the ground with as little warning as if it had been built by children out of playing cards. What was the reason? No doubt inadequate foundations were mainly responsible, but most folk preferred, in those days, to think of it as an act of God, visited upon them in protest against the burial of so unholy a man in so holy a place.

It was not long before the masons were back again to build another tower; and from then until Henry VIII's dissolution of the monasteries they and their successors were kept constantly busy as successive bishops added their own legacies to the architecture of the building. All through the Middle Ages, as the building of churches everywhere continued apace, Winchester, with its rich and ancient royal traditions, was among the leaders, passing from Norman to Early English; from Early English to Gothic.

First, King Stephen's half-brother, Henry de Blois, who died in 1171, added a treasury to the South Transept, and enriched the cathedral with many other treasures, including a font of black Tournai marble, heavily carved with emblems and figures illustrative of various myths and legends. Only seven such fonts are still in existence in this country, and Winchester's is the most perfect. At the same time he also built Farnham Castle as the bishop's palace, a purpose which it continued to serve until 1927.

Then, in the last years of the twelfth century, Bishop Godfrey de Lucy completely rebuilt the retrochoir. Where hitherto there had been only a small chapel behind the high altar, de Lucy destroyed this and, in its place, constructed an infinitely larger, though elegant, building comprising a central space with an aisle on either side and three chapels at the end.

De Lucy was prompted to take this step very largely by the ever-increasing number of pilgrims who then came to worship at the shrine of St Swithun. Religious pilgrimages became steadily more fashionable during the Middle Ages. Durham, for instance, began to attract vast crowds to the shrine of St Cuthbert, while Chichester also drew large numbers to the tomb of St Richard. To Winchester the pilgrims came from near and far in de Lucy's time in the same seemingly unending procession as they visited the shrine of the martyred St Thomas à Beckett at Canterbury. They came in sickness and in health to cure their ills, to salve their consciences, or simply to pray. Since doctors and medicine had then still a long way to go, they came perhaps most of all in sickness, hoping against hope that a touch of the shrine would cure them of their blindness, remove their lameness, or strengthen their sadly emaciated bodies.

A pitiful sight they must have made. Entering by the North Transept, whose walls were highly coloured with murals and emblems, the pilgrim bought himself a candle from the candle booth, lit it by means of a special taper, placed his taper before a picture of St Christopher (the patron saint of travellers) in thankfulness that he had come through his journey safely, dropped a coin into one of the alms-boxes if he could afford it, and took his place in the slow-moving procession as it passed up a noble flight of steps, through a canopied gateway into the presbytery aisle and on into the retrochoir.

There, in the centre of de Lucy's new building, standing upon a grey marble plinth, set on a floor that glowed red and gold and overhung by a brilliantly coloured canopy, the shrine they had tramped or hobbled so far to see now faced them – a bejewelled and ornamented, glistering casket of pure silver and gold containing the bones and dust of what had once been the body of that simple saint who had striven so earnestly to see that all this should never come about. And all around, as if to strengthen the courage and beliefs of those who came in sickness, sticks and crutches were prominently displayed as proof that others before them had arrived lame but departed cured. Sick and well alike dropped on their knees before this shrine in due turn, touched the casket with their hands – or, better still, with the afflicted portion of their body – prayed, and then departed, leaving behind them their candle and a silver piece as an offering and any other gift they might have felt able to afford to bring.

Towards the end of the fourteenth century work was begun on rebuilding the entire nave, arch by arch, bay by bay, in the Gothic style, the same stone being used throughout.

For this great enterprise two bishops were mainly responsible – William Edington, a one-time civil servant who rose to become Lord Treasurer of England and was given prefer-

The *Eclipse Inn*, Winchester, one of the oldest inns in the city, formerly St Laurence Church rectory.

Middle Gate, Winchester College, seen from Chamber Court; the original buildings of 1387-94.

Winchester College 'Sick House', built
by Warden Harris in 1656 and still
used as the Scholars' Infirmary.

The Old Chesil Rectory, dating back to the fifteenth century and
originally the rectory of old St Peter's Church.

ment in the Church as a reward for his pains, and William of Wykeham who, in those earlier days, was once employed as the latter's secretary. Edington conceived the idea of the transformation and set it in motion; but Wykeham did most of the transforming. Fortunate it was, too, that this should have proved the case. For whereas Edington appears to have been a man of but little taste and precious little understanding of architecture, Wykeham, on the other hand, possessed an unusually sound knowledge and appreciation of the subject. After knocking down the impressive Norman west front and substituting the present singularly unimpressive front, Edington had only time enough left to him before he died to do little more than reconstruct three windows, rather indifferently. Whereupon, at his death, Wykeham succeeded to the bishopric and assumed responsibility for the building operations.

Wykeham's policy was to rebuild in the Gothic style of the moment but according to the Norman plan of the past, replacing round arches with pointed and making the whole effect lighter, brighter and more delicate. He carved or refaced the heavy Norman columns and increased their height by obliterating the triforium gallery, and he gave the aisle new windows and higher vaults. But perhaps his greatest contribution was the lierne vaulting main roof with which he replaced the steep-pitched timber roof of the Normans. William of Wykeham was never to see his great work completed. The long operation continued well into the reigns of his two immediate successors, Henry Beaufort (later Cardinal) and William of Wayneflete, well into the fifteenth century, and so excellent was the design and so perfect the execution that Winchester's nave was responsible for popularizing Perpendicular architecture in England and, to this day, affords one of the finest examples of this style to be found anywhere.

Just about a hundred years after William Edington first

launched his rebuilding programme the masons began work extending the Lady Chapel at the eastern end in honour of a royal birth. On September 19th, 1486, Henry VII's consort, Queen Elizabeth, had presented the founder of the Tudor dynasty with his first son in St Swithun's priory at Winchester; and in that same year the ill-fated Prince Arthur, who later was betrothed to Catherine of Aragon but died before his sixteenth birthday, was christened in the black marble font of the cathedral, when two pipes of wine were opened in the churchyard to allow every man to drink his health.

As a thank-offering for the safe delivery of her child the queen decided to commemorate the occasion by making a gift of money to the prior for this new extension. And so Winchester's cathedral became, for a time, the longest in the world. (It is still second in length only to St Peter's, Rome.)

Bishop Richard Fox, promoted to Winchester from Exeter in 1501, then embarked upon a further programme of improvements in conjunction with the Prior of St Swithun's, Prior Silkstede. During the course of twenty-five years these two enclosed the presbytery with stone screens of lovely craftsmanship; constructed the clerestory and wooden vault of the choir; completed the exquisite reredos; and provided an east window of stained glass to give a new light and a new complexion to the entire nave.

By the time of Bishop Fox's death in 1528 Winchester was easily the richest see in England: rich enough to attract the immensely wealthy Cardinal Wolsey, whose thirst for money appears to have been insatiable, for the following year he assumed the bishopric.

Unlike his conscientious predecessors, Wolsey was interested in the see only in so far as it benefited him financially. He did not once bother to visit Winchester and, indeed, was so little concerned about his responsibilities to the place that he even detailed another to stand proxy for him at his installation. Yet he had no hesitation in spending its revenues as liberally as he pleased and upon whatever he pleased. Far from adding to the glories of the cathedral and the various monasteries, Wolsey went so far as to break up some of the smaller houses in order to add still more to the revenues at his disposal. Though he was dead within twelve months of assuming the bishopric, it was a bad twelve months for Winchester.

That year heralded the turn of the tide; the turn from prosperity to poverty.

In 1538 Thomas Cromwell sent four commissioners to Winchester to 'report'. And this is what they had to say:

Pleaseth your lordship to be advertised that this Sunday in the morning, about three of the clock, we made an end of the shrine here in Winchester. There was in it no piece of gold, nor one ring, or true stone but all great counterfeits. Nevertheless we think the silver alone thereof will amount to two thousand marks. We have also received into our possession the cross of emeralds, the cross called Jerusalem, another cross of gold, two chalices of gold, with some silver plate, parcel of the portion of the vestry; but the old prior made the plate of the house so thin that we can diminish none of it and leave the prior enything furnished. . . .

We have also this morning, going to our beds-ward, viewed the altar, which we purpose to bring with us. It will be worth taking down, and nothing thereof seen; but such a piece of work it is that we think we shall not rid it, doing our best, before Monday night or Tuesday morning, which done, we intend both at Hide and St Mary's, to sweep away all the rotten bones that be called relics; which we may not omit lest it should be thought that we came more for the treasure than for avoiding the abomination of idolatry.

47

Nor did they tell the whole tale of their vandalism. They departed with every treasure they could find – Canute's crown, the crucifixes, everything containing silver or gold or a jewel. They even made off with the brasses from some of the tombs.

A year later, in 1539, the Priory of St Swithun and the cathedral church were dissolved by Act of Parliament in company with many other religious houses.

The tide went out still farther in the Civil War when the soldiers of Oliver Cromwell stormed into Winchester and 'rode up through the body of the church and the quire until they came to the altar, where they began their work. They rudely plucked down the table and broke the rail, they threw down the organ, they broke the curiously carved work. From thence they turned to the monuments of the dead; some they utterly demolished; others they defaced. Having wreaked their fury on the beautiful chantries, they flung down several of the mortuary chests, wherein were deposited the bones of bishops, and scattered the bones all over the pavement of the church'. Many of the bones they also threw at the windows in an attempt to smash the glass, while Fox's lovely eastern window they shattered more thoroughly by striking it with the butts of their muskets. They might well have shattered William of Wykeham's chantry as well had not a staunch Wykehamist rushed into the church, sword drawn, to defend it.

Winchester Cathedral had become but a plain building, deprived of the shrine that had attracted the pilgrims over so many centuries, and empty of many of its more precious treasures. For a time the fabric itself appeared in danger of becoming ruined through neglect, until, with the Restoration, the tide began to turn slowly back again. Bit by bit the damage was made good – if not always artistically – by the restorers of the eighteenth and nineteenth centuries, and Winchester's cathedral remained among the three or four most important in the country.

Alas, another enemy that might well have proved more deadly than any of Cromwell's soldiers was at work, unseen and quite unsuspected: an enemy that went underground to strike at its very foundations. In the opening years of this century ominous cracks began to appear in walls and arches, and it was discovered that part of the floor of the building had sunk by as much as two feet. The engineer, Sir Francis Fox, called in for consultation in 1905, sank a pit to investigate the cause of the trouble – only to discover that many of the trees which Bishop Walkelin had sunk in the marshes with such care and enterprise close on 800 years ago had sunk still farther or else had disappeared entirely. As a result, parts of the walls were standing upon nothing more than peat.

What to do? There was nothing for it but to underpin the entire cathedral; and this long, laborious task was undertaken by one William Walker, a diver by trade. After the walls had been strengthened by 'grouting', the cracks being cleaned out and filled with cement, Walker excavated to a depth of many feet below the floor of the cathedral. There, deep down below the graves of the kings and bishops, he wallowed, deep in water, in the inky black, picking away at the peat with his hands. As soon as he had cleared away a pit of fair size he would place four layers of bags of cement where his peat had been and then pump out the water. Whereupon he set a series of concrete blocks above the bags, pinning each block to the masonry as he went.

Having thus strengthened one section of a wall, he proceeded to excavate a further pit. Then still more pits. So he continued for seven weary years, reinforcing the very ground upon which the cathedral stands in order that it may continue to stand for a further 800 years and more.

49

Chapter Four

THE BISHOPS OF WINCHESTER

662   Wini.

670   Leatherins.

676   Haeddi:
       Transferred the see, together with the bones of
       Birinus, from Dorchester to Winchester.

705   Daniel.

744   Hunfrith.

754   Cyneheard.

*c.*770 Aethelheard.

778   Aegbeald.

*c.*780 Cynebeorht.

*c.*802 Eahmund.

811   Wigthegn.

825   Herefirth.

*c.*835 Eadmund.

*c.*838 Eadhun.

838   Helmstan.

852   St Swithun:
       Widely beloved during his lifetime for his kind-
       ness to the sick and poor and for his generosity in
       restoring churches in the diocese at his own ex-
       pense. Naturally modest, he expressed a wish to
       be buried in the churchyard rather than in the
       building itself, but during the building of the
       second cathedral his bones were translated, an
       act which was said to have brought on a heavy
       storm, thus giving rising to the belief that if it
       rains on St Swithun's Day (July 15th) it will con-

tinue to do so for forty days. Upon the building of the present cathedral his bones were translated again, and his shrine, set in glory in the retrochoir, attracted pilgrims in great number from far and wide.

c.862   Ealhfrith.

872   Tunbeorht.

879   Denewulf.

909   Frithustan.

931   Beornstan.

934   Aelfheah I.

951   Aelfsige I.

960   Beorhthalm.

963   Aethelwold I:
Superintended the building of Winchester's second cathedral, together with conventual buildings for Benedictine monks. Upon the orders of St Dunstan, Archbishop of Canterbury, replaced the canons by monks.

984   Aelfheah II.

1006   Conwulf.

1006   Aethelwold II.

1014   Aelfsige II.

1032   Aelfwine.

1043   Stigand:
One-time chaplain to Edward the Confessor, and later Archbishop of Canterbury. Crowned King Harold, and, after the Conquest, supported Edgar Atheling. For this he was deposed by William the Conqueror. He died a prisoner at Winchester.

1073   Walkelin:
A kinsman of William the Conqueror, he became Winchester's first Norman bishop, and was responsible for the erection of the present cathedral,

the third. In order to provide adequate foundations for this he cut down trees in the surrounding royal forests, and thus earned the king's displeasure.

1107   William Giffard.

1129   Henry de Blois:

Half-brother of King Stephen, grandson of William the Conqueror, and a man of great ambition who did his best to convert the bishopric of Winchester into an Archbishopric embracing seven dioceses; a move that was nearly realized when Pope Lucius II granted a Pall. He made many gifts to the cathedral, including the font of black Tournai marble, and added a treasury. He also founded the Hospital of St Cross, a mile outside the city, which today is believed to be the oldest almshouse in the country. It was Henry de Blois who consecrated the martyr St Thomas à Beckett Archbishop of Canterbury.

1174   Richard of Ilchester.

1189   Godfrey de Lucy:

Completely rebuilt the retrochoir, setting up the shrine of St Swithun in the centre, having been prompted to take this step partly in order to provide greater accommodation for the increasing number of pilgrims to that shrine.

1205   Peter des Roches:

Has been described as the worst bishop that ever sat on the throne at Winchester. He became so immensely unpopular that he was eventually forced to leave the country in disgrace.

1244   William de Raleigh.

1250   Aymer de Valence.

1262   John Gervais.

1266   Nicholas of Ely.

1282   John of Pontoise:
        Founded St Elizabeth's College 'for the propa-
        gation of learning and piety', and was generally
        acknowledged to be a good and sound bishop.

1305   Henry Merewell.

1316   John Sandale.

1320   Rigand of Archeres.

1323   John Stratford:
        Formerly Edward II's Chancellor who aban-
        doned this post for the bishopric at the request of
        the Pope, and then became involved in the in-
        trigues that brought the king's reign to an end.

1333   Adam Orleton.

1346   William Edington:
        Began the rebuilding of the nave in the Perpen-
        dicular style and replaced the heavy Norman
        west front by the present unimpressive front. One-
        time Treasurer to Edward III, and first prelate
        of the Order of the Garter. Also served as Master
        of St Cross, and is thought to have been responsible
        for leading the thatched roof of the church there.

1367   William of Wykeham:
        Born at Wickham, near Fareham, and was edu-
        cated at Winchester's Grammar School. Was
        appointed surveyor of Windsor and other royal
        castles by Edward II. Later became the king's
        secretary, and later still Chancellor. As Chancel-
        lor he was impeached on a charge of embezzle-
        ment and dismissed from office, his estates being
        confiscated. Restored to favour, he became Chan-
        cellor for the second time. Founded New College,
        Oxford, and Winchester College, thus earning the
        title of 'Father of the Public School System'. As
        Bishop of Winchester he continued the building
        operations begun by his predecessor, and it is to

him that chief credit must be given for the present nave. By his work on that nave he established the Perpendicular style of architecture in England. He is buried in a tomb of his own design in that nave.

1404   Henry Beaufort (Cardinal):

A natural son of John of Gaunt and half-brother to Henry IV. Was awarded his Cardinal's hat by Pope Martin V. Opposed Henry V's proposition to levy a new impost on the clergy for the war against France. Sent by the Pope as legate into Germany to organize a crusade against the Hussites. In 1431 he conducted the young king, Henry VI, to Paris to be crowned King of England and France. Took part in the trial and execution of Joan of Arc. Added the Hospital of Noble Poverty to St Cross for the benefit of 'decayed noblemen'.

1447   William of Wayneflete:

Founder of Magdalen College, Oxford, Headmaster of Winchester College, first Headmaster of Eton College and later Provost of Eton.

1487   Peter Courtenay.

1493   Thomas Langton:

Appointed Archbishop of Canterbury but died of the plague before his installation.

1501   Richard Fox:

Undertook many improvements to the cathedral in conjunction with the Prior of St Swithun's, Prior Silkstede, enclosing the presbytery with stone screens, constructing the clerestory and wooden vault of the choir, completing the reredos and providing an east window of stained glass. Went blind. Founded Corpus Christi College, Oxford.

1529   Thomas Wolsey (Cardinal):

> Son of a butcher, grazier and wool merchant who rose to enjoy immense wealth and power under Henry VIII before eventually being arrested on a charge of high treason. Among the many acts for which he earned the dislike of the people was his promotion of a policy for dissolving the monasteries in order to increase the revenues of the king, various of Winchester's religious houses suffering in this way. As Bishop of Winchester he revealed no interest in the see except what he could reap from it financially. He was ordained by proxy, and never once attended the cathedral during his short term of office.

1531   Stephen Gardiner:

> At one time served as Wolsey's private secretary. Played a leading part in promoting Henry VIII's divorce from Catherine of Aragon and the downfall of Thomas Cromwell. He was despised by the Protestants for his part in sending the martyrs to the stake. Having been deprived of the see by Edward VI for refusing to comply with the king's new system of education, he was later released and was reinstated bishop by Queen Mary upon the latter's accession. Performed the marriage ceremony at the wedding in the cathedral of Queen Mary and Philip of Spain.

1551   John Ponet.

1553   Stephen Gardiner. (Restored after his deposition.)

1556   John White:

> Unpopular on account of his catholicism and deposed.

1561   Robert Horner.

1580   John Watson.

1584   Thomas Cowper.

55

1594   William Wickham.
1596   William Day.
1597   Thomas Bilson.
1616   James Montague.
1619   Launcelot Andrewes.
1627   Richard Neile.
1632   Walter Curll.
1660   Brian Duppa.
1662   George Morley:
        Built the cathedral library and rebuilt Wolvesey
        Palace. Accompanied Charles II on many of his
        travels. Was translated to Winchester from
        Worcester. At Winchester he appointed Thomas
        Ken, later to gain fame as Bishop of Bath and
        Wells, his chaplain.
1684   Peter Mews.
1707   Jonathan Trelawney:
        Completed the rebuilding of Wolvesey Palace.
1721   Charles Trimnell.
1723   Richard Willis:
        Well respected as a bishop but sometimes angered
        the Tories on account of the strong Whig bias in
        some of his sermons.
1734   Benjamin Hoadly:
        A very unpopular bishop whom George II once
        described as 'a great puppy and a very dull fellow
        and a very great rascal'. Like his predecessor, he
        too was addicted to delivering Whiggish sermons.
1761   John Thomas.
1781   Brownlow North:
        Destroyed one wing of the new Wolvesey Palace,
        built by his predecessor, Bishop Morley.
1820   George Tomline.
1827   Charles Sumner.
1869   Samuel Wilberforce.

1873   Edward Harold Browne.
1891   Anthony Wilson Thorold.
1895   Randall Thomas Davidson:
        One-time chaplain to Queen Victoria and Dean
        of Windsor. Later appointed Archbishop of Can-
        terbury and created Lord Davidson of Lambeth.
1903   Herbert Edward Ryle.
1911   Edward Stuart Talbot.
1924   Frank Theodore Woods.
1932   Cyril Forster Garbett:
        Created Archbishop of York, and later, upon the
        death of the second Archbishop Temple, was
        offered the Archbishopric of Canterbury, an
        honour which he refused on account of age.
1942   Mervyn George Haigh.
1952   Alwyn Terrell Petre Williams:
        Headmaster of Winchester College, 1924–35, and
        later Bishop of Durham.

Chapter Five

WHAT TO LOOK FOR IN THE CATHEDRAL

Second only to Westminster Abbey for its royal associations, Winchester Cathedral, architecturally, is also second only to St Peter's, Rome, as the longest church but one in Europe.

Built to the shape of a cross in the style known as Cruciform, it extends for close on 557 feet and has a breadth at the transepts of 217 feet. Yet though its walls are enriched by many attractive features in the way of flying buttresses, gargoyles, and so on, the general impression of majesty is reduced by the fact that its single tower rises to only about 138 feet and is altogether too shallow for a building of such dimensions. This deficiency seems to be accentuated by its remarkably plain west front and by its position. Through being on low ground and rather too closely surrounded by other buildings, it is impossible to obtain an overall picture of the cathedral and thus equally impossible to appreciate its true proportions. Were it to stand on a hill in full view, on the other hand, the tower would appear more lofty and the impression created would be altogether different.

Nevertheless, though the exterior tends to be a little disappointing, the interior contains a wealth of interesting architectural features, and is a treasure house of tombs, monuments, relics and other links with Winchester's historical past. Every corner has its points of interest, and the following features should be observed:

Nave and Aisles

Originally Norman, this is now of superb Gothic architecture throughout, and is said to be the finest of the kind in

England. It was through the craftsmanship in this nave that the Perpendicular style became established in England. The work of rebuilding the nave in this style was begun by Bishop William Edington, but the design was inspired, and the operation supervised, mainly by Edington's successor, William of Wykeham, Bishop of Winchester from 1367 to 1404. At the eastern end some of the original Norman columns such as once characterized the entire nave may still be seen.

The tomb of William Edington (1346–67), who began the rebuilding of the nave and designed the west front.

The tomb and chantry of William of Wykeham (1367–1404), the bishop mainly responsible for the present nave, who was also founder of Winchester College, England's first public school, and of New College, Oxford. Wykeham himself chose this spot for his tomb as it was in that very place that he used to stand to hear Mass when he was a boy. The tomb was constructed during his lifetime as an integral part of the nave, and it has been suggested that the three figures at his feet may represent the three craftsmen mainly responsible for the reconstruction of the nave.

Statues at the west end of James I and Charles I. These were executed in bronze, somewhere about 1635, by le Sueur, and were buried during the Commonwealth for safety.

A monument by Flaxman to Dr Warton, a former headmaster of Winchester College.

Grave of Jane Austen, who died at Winchester in 1817, and memorial window to her. The inscription on her tombstone reads: 'In memory of Jane Austen, youngest daughter of the late Revd. George Austen formerly Rector of Steventon in this county. She departed this life on the 15th of July, 1817 aged 41 after a long illness supported with the patience and the hopes of a Christian. The benevolence of her heart the sweetness of her temper and the extraordinary endowments

59

of her mind obtained the regard of all who knew her and the warmest love of her intimate connections. Their grief is in proportion to their affection, they know their loss to be irreparable, but in their deepest affliction they are consoled by a firm though humble hope that her charity, devotion, faith and purity have rendered her soul acceptable in the sight of her Redeemer.'

Unusual carved bosses on the balconies below the clerestory.

A twelfth-century font of black Tournai marble. This is said to be one of only seven of the kind in England and the best example now left to us. It is richly carved with emblems and figures illustrating various legends and myths, and was the gift of Bishop Henry de Blois, half-brother of King Stephen.

North Transept

A number of fine Norman pillars and arches such as once characterized the entire nave and the greater part of the cathedral are features of both the north and the south transepts.

The Epiphany Chapel with windows by Burne-Jones. This is believed to enclose the aisle where the gifts brought to the cathedral by the pilgrims to the shrine of St Swithun used to be arranged.

The Chapel of the Holy Sepulchre with the remnants of thirteenth-century murals. In the Middle Ages this was probably used only for Good Friday and Easter ceremonies.

The doorway, now blocked, through which the pilgrims entered the cathedral to worship at the shrine of St Swithun.

South Transept

The Venerable Chapel with fine Gothic screen of stone and beautiful eighteenth-century ironwork.

Prior Silkstede's Chapel containing the grave of Izaak

Walton, who died at Winchester in 1683 and who, as a memorial window shows, used to fish the River Itchen with his friend, Cotton.

The Pilgrims' Gate, a superb example of thirteenth-century ironwork, said to be the oldest of the kind in the country. This was erected largely for the control of the vast crowds that visited the cathedral to worship at St Swithun's shrine all through the Middle Ages.

An old monastic settle upon which the monks used to sit warming themselves before a charcoal fire while awaiting their turns of duty.

The Choir

Series of fourteenth-century carved stalls of Norwegian oak with fifteenth-century canopies and misericords depicting such familiar day-to-day objects as a cat with a mouse in its mouth, a sow suckling her piglets, and so on.

Sixteenth-century panels on sub-stalls, carved by Italian craftsmen. Included among the designs are the arms of Henry VIII.

The reputed tomb of William Rufus, believed to have been removed to this spot by his nephew, Bishop Henry de Blois, after the collapse of the tower. In 1868 this tomb was opened, and was found to contain the skeleton of a man of William II's stature together with fragments of gold cloth and braid of apparent Norman manufacture, various ornaments, what appeared to be an arrow-head and a number of pieces of wood which, when placed together, resembled a three-foot arrow-shaft.

Richly carved pulpit, erected by Prior Silkstede shortly before the Reformation. Skeins of silk are revealed on the panelling as a symbol of the Prior's name.

Splendid fifteenth-century reredos displaying many figures of kings and bishops who ruled or ministered at Winchester. This was erected partly in order to shut off the pilgrims visiting the shrine of St Swithun. Many of the figures were seriously mutilated or removed at the Reformation, but these have been unusually well restored or replaced, with the result that this reredos remains one of the most beautiful treasures of this or any other cathedral.

Altar rails of Charles II's time.

A number of altar books with fine red velvet bindings, presented to the cathedral by Charles II.

East window and vaulted roof of the early sixteenth century.

Presbytery

Splendid roof with wooden bosses showing the arms of Saxon and Danish kings, the arms of Henry VII, the arms of Winchester bishops, and such emblems of the Passion as the crowing cock, the three dice, the cup of vinegar, and so on.

Six mortuary chests, mounted on stone side screens of 1525, containing the bones of kings, queens and bishops, including (it is believed) those of Cynegils, England's first Christian king, who gave St Birinus the land upon which to build Winchester's first church and who died in 643; his son, Kenulph, who died in 714; Egbert, first king of all England, who died in 836; Edmund (died 946); Edred (died 955); and Canute who, according to tradition, commanded the waves at Bosham, across the Sussex border in Chichester Harbour, and who died in 1035.

The chantry of Bishop Stephen Gardiner (1531–55) containing the chair in which Mary Tudor sat during her marriage in the cathedral to Philip of Spain, the ceremony being performed by Gardiner. This bishop was despised by the Protestants of his time for his part in sending the martyrs to the stake during the Marian persecutions. Having been deprived of his see and sent to the Tower by Edward VI, he was released and reinstated Bishop of Winchester by Queen Mary. Though of historical interest, this chantry is of bad design and of no interest architecturally.

The chantry of Bishop Richard Fox (1501–28), founder of Corpus Christi College, Oxford, who effected many improvements to the cathedral.

A damaged medieval bust of the Madonna with the infant Christ.

The Retrochoir

The site and fragmentary stones of St Swithun's shrine, which was destroyed at the Reformation. By the site may be seen a Latin inscription which, when translated, reads: 'All of St Swithun that could die lay here enshrined. Hither came the faithful, not of one age or clime, to honour him with prayers and gifts. A later age laid rude hands upon his relics, but could not touch his fame. All that is of God is safe in God.' It was largely in order to accommodate the increasing number of pilgrims to this shrine that the retrochoir was constructed by Bishop Godfrey de Lucy.

The chantry of Cardinal Beaufort (1404–47) who succeeded William of Wykeham to the see of Winchester at the age of twenty-eight and was awarded his cardinal's hat by the Pope. A natural son of John of Gaunt, he lent £28,000 to Henry V, and was said to have been the wealthiest Englishman of his time.

The chantry of William of Wayneflete (1447–86), Beaufort's successor, who was one-time Headmaster of Winchester College, the first Provost of Eton College, and the founder of Magdalen College, Oxford.

The tomb of Bishop Godfrey de Lucy (1189–1205), who was responsible for the building of the retrochoir.

Three chapels at the eastern end, known as Langton's Chapel, the Lady Chapel, and the Chapel of the Guardian Angels. The southernmost of these, now the chantry of Bishop Thomas Langton (1493–1500) is believed to have been dedicated originally to St Birinus, the founder of the see, whose bones were translated to Winchester from Dorchester (Oxon) by Bishop Walkelin. The Chapel of the Guardian Angels contains a fine painted roof, and the Lady Chapel a series of fifteenth-century murals, each pointing a moral or telling a story, and some interesting woodwork.

The Crypts

An ancient well, known as the 'Ancient British Well' may be seen here; and it is possible that this was one of the wells at which the heathens of Winchester used to worship their pagan gods before the coming of Christianity and the founding of the see.

The Cathedral Library

A charter signed by Kings Ethelwulf and Alfred during their reigns at Winchester.

A tenth-century Benedictional which was produced for Bishop Aethelwold.

An eleventh-century copy of Bede.

A twelfth-century copy of the life of Edward the Confessor.

A twelfth-century Bible, written in three volumes on vellum and illuminated.

The cathedral charter of Henry V.

A number of chained books.

A medieval head of the Almighty.

Chapter Six

WINCHESTER COLLEGE

It was largely because William of Wykeham – the bishop who did so much to give the cathedral its present complexion – was born of humble, rather than rich, parents that Winchester College was founded in 1382 and opened twelve years later.

His father, John Long, and his mother, to both of whom he was devoted, were living in a small cottage in the Hampshire village of Wickham when William was born exactly seventy years previously. Having but little money, his parents sent him at a very young age to the High Grammar School of the City, which is believed to have been situated in Winchester's Little Minster Street. There he was taught his grammar and 'the three Rs'; but as Chandler, his biographer, tells us, he 'studied neither the Arts nor Theology nor yet either Canon or Civil Law'.

Since his father could not afford to send him to the university, William, upon leaving school, obtained the post of notary to the Constable of Winchester, a secretarial job that entailed recording the proceedings of councils and dispatching orders. At this he appears to have proved unusually capable, for by the age of thirty-two, he had left Winchester to take up the appointment of 'King's Clerk and Surveyor in building operations at Henley and Windsor' at a salary of a shilling a day. In one respect William of Wykeham was fortunate. The Black Death had recently taken a toll of something like 1,500,000 people in England. With more than a third of the population removed by this terrible scourge, the opportunities offered to young men of ability were naturally very

65

great. If he had been denied a great deal in the way of education, William of Wykeham evidently determined to make the most of these new opportunities.

Within a year his salary had been doubled, and by 1362 he had revealed his administrative genius in the building of the eastern wing of Windsor Castle and Queensborough Castle, and, as a result, had earned considerable fame. In that same year of 1362, on June 12th, he was ordained priest. Honours now followed in quick succession. In 1364 Edward III appointed him his private secretary and Keeper of the Privy Seal. Since it was then customary to reward outstanding ability in civil matters by granting high preferment in the Church, William of Wykeham found himself, three years later, Bishop of Winchester and Chancellor of England.

Alas, the path of success was not to continue so straight and smooth all the way. In 1376 William of Wykeham was impeached as Chancellor, whether justly or otherwise, on a charge of embezzlement. Though he had been restored to royal favour and regained his sequestrated estates within a matter of months, it was not until 1389 that he was re-appointed Chancellor.

By then he had other interests to occupy him. On his journey up that path to success Wykeham managed to amass an immense fortune in one way and another. Though it has been suggested that some of his methods of enriching himself were at least questionable and that his impeachment was probably well justified, nevertheless he had made up his mind, about the time of his ordination, to devote a part of those riches to the advancement of education. And this subject had been occupying more and more of his attention ever since.

William of Wykeham's aim was to establish two 'new colleges for poor scholars', and there to provide a system of teaching such as would equip men for the priesthood in an age when all the important posts of State were awarded to clerics and, at the same time, to supply the Church itself with men sufficiently respectable and scholarly as to be able to maintain its authority and influence at a time when the power of even the Pope seemed in danger of being challenged. The two colleges were to be complementary to one another, each being conducted independently but each having its part to play in a single scheme. Under this scheme the education of youth was to be carried out in two stages. Thus, one of the two colleges was designed as a kind of preparatory school for boys, and the other as a finishing establishment to which those same boys could then pass on in their teens to complete their education.

The second of these – the finishing college – William of Wykeham established first. Only three years after his consecration as Bishop of Winchester he bought a measure of land in the university town of Oxford, and in 1379 he founded 'New College'. Yet though the Oxford college was completed first by several years, Wykeham's preparatory institution – so important to his scheme as the school that must feed that college – also appeared in embryo at about the same time. As early as 1373 Wykeham entered into an agreement with a 'reverend and discreet gentleman master Richard de Herton, scholar' in his own cathedral city of Winchester whereby the latter agreed to undertake, for the next ten years, the teaching and instruction of all 'poor scholars whom the said Lord Bishop maintains and will continue to maintain at his own expense'. Such scholars, it seems, were housed in the parish of St John, just outside the East Gate, and attended the parish church every Sunday and feast day for their religious instruction.

Within five years of entering into this agreement William of Wykeham had sought the permission of the Pope to build a college for 'seventy poor scholars, clerks, to live college-wise and study grammar near the city of Winchester'. Before the end of 1382 he had bought the necessary land upon

67

which to build; had appointed Thomas de Cranle his first warden; and had issued a Foundation Charter giving the lands to his college. By 1388, if not before, Wykeham had drawn up his foundation statutes; and by 1394 the buildings of the new college were so far advanced as to be entered by the scholars, the Chapel, Hall and Chamber Court all being usable.

So, in the closing years of the fourteenth century, Winchester College was founded, and the first seeds of the public school tradition were sown, by a simple man who had risen from poverty to wealth and was determined that future generations should start life with greater advantages than he had enjoyed. Though Wykeham probably hoped for no more than the success of his own two colleges, his new scheme soon became a pattern. Within a few years of his death Eton College had been founded upon the same ideal as Winchester, with another future Winchester bishop, William of Wayneflete, as its headmaster. Then, in the centuries to follow, came Harrow, Charterhouse, Westminster, Rugby and many others.

Before the foundation of Winchester College – or 'St Mary Winton', as both the public school and New College, Oxford, were called originally – educational establishments fell into two groups: Cathedral and Almonry Schools, which were conducted by clerical or monastic chapters; and Grammar or High Schools, which, usually, were owned by the local corporation. The new school at Winchester, while secular, fell into neither of these categories. Though it was later to be termed a 'public school,' it was really far less 'public' than the existing schools. It was essentially a private affair, open only to boys whose parents held certain residential or other qualifications as laid down by the founder.

Under the foundation statutes the college was to comprise a warden, headmaster, usher or second master, three chaplains or 'conducts', three clerks, ten fellows, seventy scholars and sixteen quiristers, or choristers. Thus the school was open to eighty-six pupils (scholars and quiristers), who gained admission, we are told, in the following order of precedence: 'Founder's Kin' first; then natives of parishes or places in which one of the two St Mary Winton colleges has property; then natives of the diocese of Winchester; then natives of the counties of Oxon, Berks, Wilts, Somerset, Bucks, Essex, Middlesex, Dorset, Kent, Sussex or Cambridge, in order; lastly, natives of any other part of the realm of England.

Relatives of the founder, besides enjoying priority of election, were given various other privileges. They could enter the school at the youthful age of seven and remain there, if their parents wished, until they were twenty-five. If they proved backward in their work, they were to receive special coaching from one of the chaplains, for which services the latter were to be paid an extra six shillings and eightpence a year; and they could engage and maintain their own personal servants in college. The ordinary scholars were accepted at the age of eight, and were required to pass on to New College as soon as they reached their teens (provided, of course, that they were able to gain their election); and they enjoyed no special rights. The quiristers came into a very much lower category. Invariably of poor parentage, they were admitted to the school solely on the strength of their voices, which had to be sufficiently melodious to qualify them to sing in the chapel choir. And far from being allowed servants, they themselves were required to wait in hall and to make the beds of the Fellows and undertake various other menial duties.

Apart from the quiristers, who wore special uniforms and had their own quarters, these pupils, or 'scholars', were all housed together in college.

While Wykeham planned his school mainly for the benefit of his own kith and kin and for the sons of men whose annual income did not exceed five marks, or £3 6s 8d, this arrangement was not to remain undisturbed for long. So novel a system of education, practised in a royal town that was also the seat of the richest bishopric, was bound to attract attention. It attracted the nobility, from the king downwards. Henry VI paid several visits to the college, and it was as a result of these visits that Eton was founded. Many years before that, however, only very shortly after Wykeham's death in 1404, certain noblemen were sufficiently impressed to wish their own sons to avail themselves of these new opportunities, and were approaching the headmaster requesting him to accept their boys 'by private arrangement' upon the payment of agreed fees. Finding his modest salary of £10 a year wholly inadequate, the headmaster required little tempting, and agreed readily.

In order to distinguish them from the scholars provided for under the foundation statutes, these fee-paying sons of the gentry were known as 'commoners'. If their parents lived locally they boarded at home and attended the school as day boys, otherwise they were accommodated at their fathers' expense in various buildings in the town. So successful did this experiment prove that before long the number of commoners had exceeded the number of scholars. Nevertheless their acceptance into the school continued to be a matter of private arrangement between headmaster and parents until 1870, and nearly all the buildings provided specifically for their use were acquired or built by private initiative.

Thus, as far back as the fifteenth century, Winchester College began to assume its present character.

Life, however, was very different in those days. The school year consisted of only two terms instead of three – 'Long Half', from mid-January to mid-July; and 'Short Half', from about mid-September until Christmas. Virtually the only subjects taught were Latin, Greek and a little simple arithmetic, but the programme of work must have appeared stupendous to all but the most brilliant and natural of scholars.

Every day the boys had to be out of their beds by 5.30 a.m. and in chapel by 6 o'clock. On four days of the week they then had to do three hours' work on an empty stomach in 'school'. Here, in one restricted room, the entire school worked together. The headmaster shouted at his particular class in one corner, while the second master bawled as determinedly at his charges at the other end; and the sleepy pupils rubbed their eyes and yawned as they did their best to concentrate upon their lessons in all the noise. At the end of this long and tediously protracted period the boys were allowed a bare half-hour for a breakfast of 'bread, stinking butter, and beer or milk'. By 10.30 a.m. they had to be at their desks, or 'scobs', once more, and there they remained until about midday when they were given a short break before lunch. No sooner had they swallowed the last mouthful of this meal than again they had to be in school. Except for a short interval of a quarter of an hour for 'bevers' of bread and beer, this stretch of lessons lasted for four hours: four deadly hours of learning Latin or Greek by heart, translating, or composing verses in those languages.

At 6 o'clock came the main meal of the day – 'a cut off the joint, mouldy bread and beer' on most days, according to one pupil. Beer was served freely at all schools in those days because the local water supply was generally infected and dangerous, and it was considered simpler and cheaper to brew beer than purify water. After dinner there was preparation work to see to; and the day ended with a chapel service. Soon after 9 o'clock each evening the boys were in bed.

To bed – but not necessarily to sleep. Often the boys found that they were unable to get through all their preparation work for the following day unless they worked well into the night by the light of a tallow candle that stood on a shelf at the head of their beds. Sometimes they were obliged to rise before the usual waking hour, perhaps as early as 3 a.m. On such occasions they would guard against oversleeping by

71

leaving their candles alight all night and fixing a kind of booby trap whereby as soon as the wicks burnt down to a certain level the flames ignited strings and thus released a pile of books on to the sleeper's head.

Though not every day was quite so exacting, every day brought its quota of beatings and bullyings. The headmaster appeared daily in 'school', dressed in cocked hat and gown, to give anything up to fifty strokes with a rod of apple twigs on the bared backs of wrongdoers, often for the most seemingly trivial of crimes. At the same time some of the older boys bullied the younger ones mercilessly. It appears to have given a bully particular pleasure to roast a junior before a roaring fire until he fainted; to draw a red-hot stick across the backs of his hands; or to toss him in blankets on to the stone floor. As a test to see whether a new boy was 'of Founder's Kin' – one of tough Wykehamical stock – the bully was also particularly fond of beating his culprit on the head with a bread trencher to see which broke first, the trencher or his head.

The masters themselves were often not much better. True to the traditions of the times, they often went out of their way to make their pupils frightened of them in the belief that such tactics helped them to maintain authority; and it is recorded that more than one master was known, in the eighteenth century, to break a cricket stump in two across the back of a boy who had failed to do well in his work.

Though the programme was unduly arduous for the greater part of the week, on Tuesdays and Thursdays the boys were free nearly all day to do much as they pleased. Since organized sport was then still a thing of the future, they spent those welcome leisure hours playing a rough-and-ready form of cricket or football; fighting schoolboy battles on St Catherine's Hill, known to the Wykehamists as 'Hills'; bathing in the river; or hunting the badger. But as nobody, least of all the masters, cared very much what they did, some of the more dissolute boys preferred to idle away their time drinking.

Such was life at Winchester right down to the middle of the nineteenth century; and, for all its shortcomings, it was a cleaner form of life than that to be found in most schools of that time. Throughout that long period, during which so many other schools were modelling themselves upon William of Wykeham's college, the original foundation statutes maintained unaltered, and were sworn to by every pupil as soon as he reached the age of fifteen.

Then, in the first half of the nineteenth century the entire public school system changed its complexion – thanks to one of Winchester's most famous pupils, Dr Thomas Arnold, who entered the school as a commoner in 1807 and then transferred the following year to college where he remained as a scholar until 1811. During the years 1828 to 1842, when he died at the still youthful age of forty-seven, Dr Arnold laboured, as headmaster of Rugby, to abolish the bullyings and brutality which then beset the life of all schools by making Christianity the basis of his entire educational system and by developing a new kind of prefectorial system such as gave the boys a measure of self-government and a greater sense of responsibility. By his numerous innovations, not least of which was his introduction of the house system – today an essential part of the public school tradition – he became as much 'the father of the modern public school', as he is called, as William of Wykeham was the father of the old.

In the decades following Dr Arnold's death schools everywhere began to remould themselves upon the Rugby pattern, while a large number of new ones were also founded in accordance with his ideas. With the face of education changing so generally it was natural that Winchester should change too; and Dr Moberly, who was headmaster of the college at the time and who had taught Matthew Arnold for a year, was the first to admit that he had studied Dr Arnold's methods carefully and that he had been influenced considerably by the latter in his own work at Winchester.

Any trend towards more modern ideals which Moberly may have encouraged was given more permanent shape and form in 1857. In that year the Oxford University Commissioners arrived to study conditions at Winchester; and in that year the very statutes changed. The entire management of the school, we are told, was overhauled, and the teaching placed on a new footing.

With the appointment of Dr Ridding as headmaster nine years later the changes became 'numerous, swift and radical'. The number of entries to the school increased sensationally, and houses such as Dr Arnold had established at Rugby were set up to accommodate the overflow of commoners. Instead of the boys learning their lessons together in an atmosphere of pandemonium in 'school', each form was now given its 'div-room' where it could concentrate in quiet. The prefectorial system – where hitherto boys had been given certain privileges without being required to assume any responsibilities – was remodelled upon the Arnold pattern, and ruthless war was declared against the bullying and the many other vices that had characterized the Winchester of old. At the same time organized sport took its rightful place in the programme of school life.

Long before the nineteenth century was out Winchester had acquired most of its present characteristics, and had become indeed a school where 'manners makyth man'.

Chapter Seven

THE WARDENS AND HEADMASTERS
OF WINCHESTER COLLEGE

Wardens

1382   Thomas de Cranle of Cranleigh, Surrey:
> Created Archbishop of Dublin. Appointed Chancellor by Henry IV and made Justiciary of the Realm by Henry V. Refused a Cardinal's hat offered by the Pope.

1389   John Westcott.

1393   John Morys of Gloucestershire.

1413   Robert Thurbern of Southampton:
> Left property to the school to celebrate his death. A chantry was built to his memory to the south side of the school chapel.

1450   Thomas Chandler of Wells:
> Served a term as Secretary of State. Was appointed warden of New College, Oxford.

1454   John Baker of Aldermaston, Berks:
> Rebuilt the tower of Thurbern's chantry.

1487   Michael Clyve of St Ebbs, Oxon.

1501   John Rede of Kingsley, Hants.

1520   Ralph Barnacke of Alresford, Hants.

1526   Edward More of Havant, Hants.

1545   John White of Farnham, Surrey:
> Assisted as confessor to Catherine Howard. Created Bishop of Lincoln. Preached funeral sermon at the burial of Queen Mary, praising the work of the dead queen in the presence of Queen

Elizabeth I. For this and other acts, he gained Elizabeth's displeasure, and was sent to the Tower, but was later released. Bequeathed his mitre and crozier to the college.

1554 John Boxall of Bramshott.

1556 Thomas Stempe of Winchester.

1580 Thomas Bilson of Winchester:
One of the most eminent of Elizabethan divines. Preached the consecration sermon at the coronation of James I. Assisted Dr Miles Smith with his translation of the Bible. As warden he limited the number of pupils eligible at any one time for entry to the college under Founder's Kin. He was the first warden to marry, it having been previously taken for granted that the warden should be celibate. His marriage made new building operations necessary. Was buried in Westminster Abbey.

1596 John Harmer of Newbury, Berks:
One of the translators of the Authorized Version of the Bible.

1613 Nicholas Love of Froxfield, Hants.

1630 John Harris of Hardwick, Bucks:
Generally regarded as the greatest warden of all time. To him fell the task of keeping the school on a sound footing during the troublous days of the Civil War, and a brass in Cloisters records that 'in the difficult whirlpool of that age he guided through many a storm, with God's help, the ship of which he was captain'. Built part of Sick House.

1658 William Burt of Winchester.

1679 John Nicholas of West Dean, Sussex:
Made improvements in the college chapel. Was largely responsible for Wren being commissioned to build School. Added to the warden's lodgings,

Commoner Gate, Winchester College War Memorial Cloister.

The Town Mill and city bridge. The Mill is National Trust property, and is now used as a youth hostel.

'School', Winchester College, built in 1683–7, where the entire school once worked together. In the background, Fromond's Chantry (c. 1425–45) appears over the old cloisters, which were consecrated in 1395.

contributing generously to the cost out of his own pocket.

1711   Thomas Braithwaite of Enham, Hants.

1720   John Cobb of Adderbury.

1724   John Dobson of Chiddesden.

1729   Henry Bigg of Chilton Foliat, Berks.

1740   John Coxed of Bucknell.

1757   Christopher Golding of Midhurst, Sussex.

1763   Harry Lee of Coton, Salop.

1789   George Isaac Huntingford of Winchester:
During his wardenship several school 'rebellions' occurred during one of which he was barricaded in his own house. He was generally regarded as an extremely bad warden, and gained the name of 'Old Corruption'. His forty-two-years' reign at Winchester were in every way disastrous. Nevertheless he was rewarded at the end with the appointment of Bishop of Gloucester. Later he was transferred to Hereford.

1832   Robert Specott Barter of Cornworthy:
In conjunction with Headmaster Moberly he did much to stamp out the barbarisms that were so manifest under the reign of his predecessor, above all breaking down the traditional barrier between scholars and commoners.

1861   Godfrey Bolles Lee of Froyle:
The last resident warden. Upon his death, in 1903, it was decided to abolish the post as such in favour of non-resident wardens, appointed under fresh regulations.

1903   Sir Kenneth Muir-Mackenzie.

1915   James Parker Smith, P.C.

1920   William Waldegrave Palmer, 2nd Earl of Selborne, K.G.

1925   Sir Frederick George Kenyon, G.B.E.

1930   Frederick John Napier Thesiger, 3rd Baron and
       1st Viscount Chelmsford, G.C.S.I.

1932   Sir Oswald Richard Arthur Simpkin, K.C.B.,
       C.B.E., M.A.

1936   Harold Trevor Baker, P.C., M.A.

1946   Gavin Turnbull Simonds, Baron Simonds, P.C.

1951   Sir George Henry Gates, G.C.M.G., K.C.B.,
       D.S.O.

Headmasters

1373   Richard de Herton of Winchester:
       Undertook by private arrangement with William
       of Wykeham, before the foundation of the col-
       lege, to teach and instruct for ten years all the
       'poor scholars whom the said Lord Bishop main-
       tains and will continue to maintain at his own
       expense'.

1388   John Melton:
       One-time Master of the local Hospital of St Mary
       Magdalen. Believed to have been indicted for
       stealing thirteen pieces of cloth to the value of £7.

1394   Thomas Rumsey.

1407   John Pole.

1414   Thomas Romsey.

1418   Richard Darcy.

1424   Thomas Alwin of Estford, Lincs.

1430   William of Wayneflete:
       One of the greatest of all Winchester's head-
       masters. Later became, in turn, Headmaster of
       Eton, Provost of Eton.

1441   Thomas Alwin.

1444   William Ive.

1454   John Bernard of Over Wallop, Hants.

1459   John Grene of Chilcombe, Dorset.

1464   Clement Smith of Southwark:
           One-time Headmaster of Eton and Canon of
           Windsor.

1467   Richard Dene of Hambledon:
           Later became Archbishop of Canterbury.

1484   John Rede of Kingsley, Surrey.

1490   Robert Festham of Vernham.

1495   William Horman of Salisbury:
           One-time Headmaster of Eton and Vice-Provost
           of Eton. Author of *Vulgaria*.

1501   John Farlington of Smithfield, London.

1507   Edward More of Havant, Hants.

1515   Thomas Erlisman of Gatcombe, Isle of Wight.

1525   John Twychener of Wokingham, Berks.

1531   Richard Twychener of Wokingham.

1535   John White of Farnham, Surrey.

1541   Thomas Bailey of Portisham, Dorset.

1546   William Evered of Dorset.

1553   Thomas Hide of Newbury, Berks.

1561   Christopher Johnson of Derby.

1571   Thomas Bilson of Winchester.

1579   Hugh Lloyd of Carnarvon:
           One-time Canon of St Paul's.

1588   John Harmar of Newbury, Berks.

1596   Benjamin Heyden of Winchester.

1602   Nicholas Love of Froxfield, Hants.

1613   Hugh Robinson of Anglesey.

1627   Edward Stanley of Chichester.

1643   John Potenger of Burghfield, Berks.

1653   William Burt of Winchester.

1658   Henry Beeston of Titchfield, Hants.

1679   William Harris of Colerne, Wilts:
           A great benefactor to both the college and the
           cathedral.

1700   Thomas Cheyney of Titcombe, Wilts:
       One-time Dean of Lincoln and Dean of Winchester.

1724   John Burton of Keresley, Warwick:
       Founded Commoners' College where he encouraged an aristocratic tone, arranging for the portraits of his titled pupils to be hung in what is now the Second Master's dining-room. Despite his snobbish tendency, he is generally regarded as the greatest headmaster since Wayneflete.

1766   Joseph Warton of Dunsfold, Surrey:
       One-time Canon of St Paul's.

1793   William Stanley Goddard:
       A great benefactor who, in 1834, invested £25,000 for the college to advance the stipends of the headmaster and usher. Among his pupils was Dr Thomas Arnold, the great headmaster of Rugby and educational reformer. One-time Canon of St Paul's.

1810   Henry Dixon Gabell of Winchester:
       A great scholar but almost universally disliked by his pupils. He also taught Dr Arnold.

1824   David Williams of Lasham, Hants.

1836   George Moberly of St Petersburg:
       In his conduct of the school he was strongly influenced by the example of Dr Arnold, three of whose sons were at one time his pupils. Following Arnold's lead, he introduced the house system; and he founded New Commoners. Supported by Warden Barter, he did much to abolish the old barbarisms, reducing the average weekly 'Biblings' from 150 to three. Through the combined efforts of Moberly and Barter the whole moral tone of the school improved enormously. He was later appointed Bishop of Salisbury.

1866   George Ridding of Winchester:
        One of the greatest of Winchester's headmasters
        who reformed the school so widely that he is
        known as the Second Founder. He spent more
        than £20,000 on his material improvements,
        nearly half of which he paid for out of his own
        pocket. Following Moberly's lead, he opened six
        new houses. He later became first Bishop of
        Southwell.

1884   William Andrewes Fearon of Assington.

1901   Hubert Murray Burge of Meerut, India.
        Gained the appointment after serving as Head-
        master of Repton for two terms. Later became
        Bishop of Southwark and Bishop of Oxford.

1911   Montague John Rendall:
        Superintended the building of War Cloister, con-
        sulting with the architect and workman regularly
        and visiting the operations daily.

1924   Alwyn Terrel Petre Williams:
        Later became Bishop of Durham, but in 1952
        was transferred to the See of Winchester.

1935   Spencer Leeson:
        Later became Bishop of Peterborough.

1946   Walter Oakeshott.
        Later appointed Rector of Lincoln College,
        Oxford.

1954   Henry Desmond Pritchard Lee.

Chapter Eight

THE WYKEHAMISTS' VOCABULARY

EVERY public school has its list of peculiar words and phrases but it is doubtful if any has a larger vocabulary than Winchester. Below is a selection of some of the more unusual expressions that are used today or else have been in use during the last hundred years.

Baker:

A comfortable seat.

Battlings:

The weekly pocket money allowance of a shilling paid to the boys at school.

Beeswaxers:

Heavy boots.

Bevers:

An allowance of beer that used to be served to the boys during break time.

Bibling:

A form of punishment where the headmaster appeared daily in School, dressed in cocked hat and gown, to give anything up to fifty strokes with a rod of apple twigs on the bared backs of wrongdoers.

Blow:

To blush with embarrassment.

Boner:

A rap on the spine.

Books-Chambers:

Preparation work.

Brock:

To tease.

Brum:
  Penniless.
Bulky:
  Good-natured.
Candle-Keeper:
  The name given to each of the seven most senior juniors, or Inferiors, who were exempt from fagging.
Cargo:
  A food parcel from home.
Chisel:
  To cheat.
Chouse:
  A school scandal.
Continent:
  To fall sick.
Domum:
  The call made by the Prefect of Hall when summoning the boys to return from their play on 'Hills'.
Extrumps:
  To construe in class without having previously learnt the lesson.
Finge:
  The word used instead of 'feigns' when trying to avoid undertaking an unpleasant task.
Founder's Comm.:
  The four days in the year set aside for the commemoration of the foundation of the college.
Founder's Ob.:
  The day of the commemoration of the Founder's death.
Frowt:
  Angry.
Furk:
  Expel.
Gated:
  Confined within the college gates.

Gomer:

A new hat.

Gown:

Brown paper when particularly substantial.

Highlows:

A peculiar type of football shoe once worn.

Hiss:

A call made by a junior when ordered to keep watch against the approach of a master. In the old days a prefect would often detail a junior to keep watch in this way when engaged in an unlawful game of five-card loo.

Huff:

A form of ale that used to be brewed by the college authorities in the days when it was unsafe to drink the local water.

Inferior:

The name given to every boy who was not a prefect.

Jack:

A leather can in which the beer used to be served.

Jawster:

One who talked too much.

Jubilee:

A holiday or other occasion for rejoicing.

Junket:

To boast.

Kid:

Cheese.

Launch:

To drag a boy from his bed, together with his mattress and bedclothes, on to the floor.

Lobster:

To cry or 'blub'.

Luxer:

A good-looking boy.

Mons:

A crowd.

Muttoner:

A blow from a cricket ball which removes the skin from the knuckles.

Nestor:

A boy who failed to make the necessary grade in the school commensurate with his age or physique.

Percher:

A form of cross written against the name of a boy absent from chapel or any other school activity without leave.

Pitch-up:

To make friends.

Pruff:

Obstinate.

Purler:

A dive into the water when bathing.

Rabbiter:

A blow on the back of the neck delivered with the edge of the open hand.

Remedy:

A holiday from work, a term derived from 'remission day'.

Roker:

A stick or implement used for stirring.

Scaldings:

A warning cry used by the boys when their fellows appeared to be in any form of danger or risk.

Scob:

A kind of play-box designed for use as a desk and for the storage of books and other things.

Scrape Out:

A term used in connection with a prefect wishing to leave the school-room. Such a boy would stand near the door and scrape with his feet to attract his master's attention. The master then nodded his consent.

Scrubbing:
A flogging comprising four strokes, or 'cuts'.

Scrutiny:
An inquiry under the Foundation Statutes held by the Warden of New College and Posers of the seven seniors and seven juniors in college as to whether they have any complaints to make against conditions in college.

Semper Testis:
A boy who is willing to bear testimony for one of his companions in the case of an inquiry.

Settler:
A form of repartee that leaves nothing more to be said.

Sines:
The allowance of bread issued to the boys at breakfast and supper.

Skirmish:
A form of cross-country run particularly popular in the old days before the development of organized sport.

Sock:
To hit hard or defeat.

Socius:
A companion. This word was used particularly in the old days in reference to a boy who accompanied another to St Catherine's Hill, or 'Hills'.

Speg:
Smart, a term once used in reference to a boy who dressed well.

Splice:
To throw.

Squish:
Weak tea.

Stuckling:
A form of pudding comprising chopped meat and apple, the whole flavoured with carraway. This was eaten at special dinners such as Election Dinner.

Sus:

The leavings of the seniors' tea which the juniors used to eat.

Thick:

Dense.

Thoke:

Idle. The word was not used only in a bad sense. On certain occasions a boy could obtain permission to lie in bed later than usual; and such permission was termed a 'hatch thoke'.

Tight:

An adjective used in the sense of firm or confirmed. A boy who was a snob, for instance, would often be called a 'tight snob'.

Tin Gloves:

A term used by the old-time bullies. A new boy would be asked if he had brought his tin gloves to school with him. When the latter showed that he did not understand the question the bully would take a red-hot stick from the fire and draw six lines across the back of each hand, adding, as he did so, that his hands would now be so tough as to no longer need gloves, tin or otherwise.

Toys:

A desk fitted with a cupboard and bookshelf for use in a study.

Toy-Time:

Evening preparation work.

Tug:

Stale news.

Tund:

To beat on the back with a stick.

Valet:

A kind of fag responsible for looking after the clothes of a scholar.

Vessel of Paper:
A quarter sheet of foolscap paper.

Warden's Child:
A boy selected each year by the Warden for the enjoyment of certain privileges.

Warden's Prog.:
The annual visit of the Warden and Bursar to inspect the college estates.

Washing Stool:
A special kind of table with four outward-slanting legs used by the prefects.

Worsteders:
Thick worsted stockings that used to be worn outside the trousers at football to act as shin pads.

Chapter Nine

WHAT TO LOOK FOR IN
WINCHESTER COLLEGE

BEING the oldest of our public schools, and having been founded by a man with an unusually sound appreciation of architecture, who, as we have seen, had already won considerable renown through his handling of the building operations at Windsor Castle and Queensborough Castle, Winchester College possesses a fine range of medieval buildings and some of the most perfect architecture to be found at any school in England.

The original building activities began in 1387 and continued until shortly after 1400; and the work was carried out according to the designs of William Wynford, a master mason whom William of Wykeham also commissioned to rebuild the nave of the cathedral and his college at Oxford, and who was responsible for the beautiful western towers of Wells Cathedral and the defences of Southampton. It was at Windsor that Wykeham and Wynford first met in 1360 when the future bishop was Clerk of the Works and the mason was employed as one of the king's master craftsmen; there that the two began their great partnership. As might be expected, therefore, elements of the Windsor Castle plan appear again at Winchester.

Happily, the architectural interest is not restricted only to the Middle Ages, however. The splendid tradition begun by William of Wykeham has been maintained unusually well through the centuries by his successors. No less a figure than Sir Christopher Wren is believed to have supplied the plans and designs for at least one of the seventeenth-century buildings; while such twentieth-century buildings as Commoner Gate, commemorating Wykehamists who fell in the South African War, and the still more modern war memorial to the memory of those who died in the 1914–18 war (both erected at a period when architecture generally left much to be desired) are real works of art. Thus, while the medieval still predominates, buildings of many periods are seen companioning Wykeham's and Wynford's work; and, in the main, they are seen as sympathetic and worthy companions.

The following are some of the more interesting features:

College Wall

The approach to the school is, in itself, of considerable interest, for it will be noticed that the college wall, to the south of College Street, is pierced by a number of small windows of the fourteenth century besides a number of larger ones. The smaller are all original, and they recall the fact that when William of Wykeham founded his college in 1382 the Peasants' Revolt, when the 'unfree' orders of society, led by Wat the Tyler and John Ball, marched against the lords of the manors, murdering and pillaging as they went, was only a year old. Since Wykeham also had vivid memories of the bloody conflict of Town and Gown which took place in Oxford in 1355, he wisely arranged for his Winchester college, like his college at Oxford, to assume something of the character of a fort with a strong outer wall that would prove capable of withstanding the worst assault.

Outer Gate

This gate leads from the street into the Outer Court of the college. On its north face is a fine statue of the Virgin and Child which has been described as 'one of the masterpieces of medieval English sculpture'. The statue dates from about 1394 when the tower was constructed and probably owes its splendid state of preservation to the fact that it was originally painted. The detail in the Child's face, with its smiling countenance, provides an unusual example of fourteenth-century realism. Another feature of the gate is an interesting star vault containing a grotesque head with inlaid eyes and an expression that changes according to the angle from which it is approached. To the arriving visitor it appears to beam a friendly welcome, but to the departing it throws a gloomy and depressed look.

Chamber Court

A further gate leads from Outer Court into Chamber Court, a beautiful quadrangle that can have changed but little since the fourteenth and fifteenth centuries. The centre of college life from the beginning, it is here in the buildings surrounding this quadrangle that the seventy scholars on the foundation have always lived and worked. Each of the various chambers was provided for a specific purpose. Election Chamber with the room above were earmarked for the warden, and there were separate rooms for the usher. The fellows lived three or four together in their rooms, while a single chamber had to suffice for the sixteen quiristers. Seventh Chamber served as the original schoolroom, and it was here that the headmaster and usher used to conduct their respective classes at opposite ends before the seventeenth-century 'school' was built. It is thought that Seventh Chamber is probably the oldest schoolroom to survive to the present day.

Hall

On the south side of Chamber Court, immediately above Seventh Chamber, is Hall, an impressive room with a timber roof of original design which was almost entirely renewed in 1820. Here may be seen the old wooden trenchers used by the boys at their meals and an interesting collection of portraits. The most notable of these are a 1597 pastiche of the founder (the earliest in existence) by Sampson Strang, alias Starkey of Oxford; and a painting of John Potenger, who was head-master of the college from 1643 to 1653.

Near the foot of the steps down from the hall is a small ves-tibule leading to the kitchen; and here will be found another painting, the famous *Trusty Servant*. This is the work of John Hoskyns, a scholar of 1580, who later became a Serjeant-at-law, and it portrays a figure that is half human and half animal, an idea that has been traced back to early fourteenth-century French art.

Chapel

Though the Chapel (also to the south of Chamber Court) was first used by the scholars as long ago as 1394, when Wykeham's pupils first went into occupation, the tower or belfry was constructed about a hundred years later. With its walls once adorned with murals and its windows glazed with splendid medieval stained glass, the building must have been extremely colourful in the days before the Reformation. Though such splendour has never been restored – and never could be – the chapel still contains many remarkable fea-tures. The vault, of quasi-fan design, is original, and was designed by none other than Hugh Herland, the king's chief carpenter, who, only a year or two later, achieved his crown-ing glory by designing the splendid roof of Westminster Hall. The seats of the stalls, together with their misericords, are also original, the best examples being the second from the west on the north side and the second from the east on the south side. The reredos too, carefully restored by William Butterfield, is fifteenth-century work; as also are the sedilia.

The stained glass we see today is a reasonably accurate copy of the original design; and it was executed in 1821–8 by Betton and Evans of Shrewsbury, the pioneers in unravelling the lost secrets of medieval glass painting. Yet the colouring, and indeed the whole effect, is unconvincing and does not

The house in College Street where Jane Austen died.

The City Cross, Winchester, erected at the time of Henry VI, showing the Pentice beyond.

The Beaufort Tower, St Cross Hospital. The hospital was founded by Bishop Henry de Blois in about 1133.

Cheyney Court, one of Winchester's oldest houses, and Close Gate.

bear comparison with the original. Fortunately, not all of the original glass is lost to Winchester. The glass from the east 'Jesse' window has survived, and this has been restored and placed in the west window of the south side chapel, known as Thurbern's Chantry.

This chantry, called after Robert Thurbern, who was warden from 1413 to 1450 and left property to the school to celebrate his death or 'obit.', was added between 1478 and 1485; and it was then that the bell tower was built, though this has since been rebuilt of the original stone. The vault of this chapel, with its carved stone bosses, is original, and is thought to be the work of the same craftsmen as carved the slightly earlier vault of the Divinity School at Oxford, which was designed by Master William Orchard.

Cloisters

South of the chapel are the Cloisters. These, too, form part of the original fabric, and in the Middle Ages it was customary for the fellows of the college to be buried here, a special 'bull' having been obtained from the Pope to allow this. In summer they were also used – as were the cloisters of many of the medieval monasteries – for study purposes. It is possible that the various feast-day processions likewise took place here, as was the practice in the cloisters of Wykeham's college at Oxford.

Fromond's Chantry

This chapel, close by the cloisters, was built between 1420 and 1445 by the executors of John Fromond, steward of the Hampshire and Wiltshire manors, who left property to the school for the singing of Masses for his soul; a common form of bequest in that highly superstitious age. The upper floor was intended to serve as a library for the fellows, and in recent years it has been restored for similar purpose, now housing the 'Wiccamica' collection of books and documents relating to the history of the college. The chapel fell into disuse in the sixteenth century under an Act of Parliament, introduced in the reign of Edward VI, suppressing the chantries. Since the latter part of the last century, however, it has been used as a kind of overflow chapel for boys in their first year at school, thus easing congestion in the main chapel, which is too small to accommodate present numbers.

School

To the south-west of the cloisters is School. This was built in 1683-7 to take the place of the original schoolroom in Seventh Chamber which, in view of the steadily increasing number of commoners, had by then grown far too small to accommodate the pupils. It was in this building that Dr Thomas Arnold, the great reforming headmaster of Rugby and the 'father of the modern public school', learnt his lessons.

It is thought that the designs for this imposing building were supplied by Sir Christopher Wren during the time that he was working in the city building a new royal palace for Charles II and the Palace of Wolvesey for Bishop Morley. The hall certainly bears a distinct Wren 'flavour', and its mellow brickwork tones beautifully against the lovely old stone of the main buildings.

War Memorials

Winchester's two war memorials afford a splendid example of the way in which modern buildings can be produced in harmony with the old. War Cloister, enclosing a well-kept grass sward, was opened in 1924 to commemorate those who were killed in the 1914-18 war. It was designed by the late Sir Herbert Baker and must surely rank among the most beautiful and peaceful memorials to the fallen to be found anywhere in the country. Leading from this cloister is the second memorial, Commoner Gate, built to the memory of

Wykehamists who fell in the South African War. This, too, is well in keeping with the school's fine architectural tradition.

Sickhouse

Beyond the war memorials, on the way down to the 1st XI cricket grounds, is yet another interesting building, College Sickhouse, a charming specimen of Commonwealth domestic architecture, erected in 1656 of rosy red brick. Many famous Wykehamists have been nursed back to health in this attractive little building. Dr Arnold himself once retired there shamming earache when he found the work too much for him – but, alas, only to be dismissed forthwith and severely admonished by the headmaster, Dr Goddard, as soon as the sham was detected.

Chapter Ten

ST CROSS

WHILE one of Winchester's bishops set himself the task of educating the needy for the Church by founding a school that was to provide the seed-bed for a new tradition, another, Henry de Blois, had already established, nearly two hundred years previously, a home in the city for those of 'the poor of Christ' who, far from looking forward into the future like Wykeham's youths, were now looking sadly back over the past.

Possibly some such establishment had already existed in the capital many years before de Blois' time; if so, it had sadly decayed, or else ceased to exist altogether. The plight of the poor was terrible in the twelfth century, for, says a contemporary writer, 'then was corn dear, and flesh, and cheese, and butter, for there was none in the land: wretched men starved with hunger – some lived on alms who had been erstwhile rich. . . . The earth bare no corn; one might as well have tilled the sea. . . . It was said openly that Christ and His saints slept'.

For the old, conditions were particularly testing; so that in the year 1136 Bishop Henry de Blois decided to found the Hospital of St Cross for the benefit of 'thirteen poor men, feeble and so reduced in strength that they can hardly or with difficulty support themselves without another's aid'. Here, at St Cross, each was to be provided with a comfortable bed and clothes and served daily with good wheaten bread to the weight of five marks with 'three dishes at dinner and one at supper suitable to the day, and drink of good stuff'.

Besides catering for the thirteen inmates, the hospital was to give a daily dinner to a hundred other 'poor and indigent men', and to dispense hospitality to the poor generally in so far as their finances would allow. In order to raise those funds the bishop appropriated the tithes of twelve of the parishes in his diocese as well as those of further parishes in the two dioceses of Salisbury and Lincoln.

Fifteen years after founding his almshouse Bishop Henry de Blois entrusted its management to the care of the Knights of St John of Jerusalem. Thereafter the power of management passed to and fro between the Hospitallers and the Bishop of Winchester before being finally assigned to the bishop in 1200.

By then de Blois was dead and the hospital had expanded. In 1174 Richard of Ilchester had succeeded to the See of Winchester, and had decided to extend the founder's good work by allowing a further hundred poor men to receive their daily dinner at St Cross. Whereupon the hospital staff was increased to include, besides the Master, four priests, thirteen secular clerks and a number of choristers, all of whom were to be paid for their services partly in beer and meat. What payment such officers received in the way of money in those days is not recorded, but it seems that in 1350 the Master was receiving eight pounds and each of the four priests thirteen shillings and fourpence a year, while the less fortunate choristers were obliged to subsist very largely upon the food which the Master and Brethren left on their tables at the end of their meals.

In establishing St Cross Henry de Blois intended to cater only for poor folk of humble birth. In 1446, however, when his long reign as bishop was drawing to its close, Cardinal Henry Beaufort, half-brother of Henry IV and said to have been the richest Englishman of his day, decided that the time had come to do something for impoverished gentlefolk as well: for men who, in their younger days, 'had everything handsome about them' but who had since suffered serious reverses.

With this idea in mind, Beaufort added to the foundation of St Cross a second foundation to be known as 'The Almshouse of Noble Poverty' where thirty-five noblemen, or men who had been in the Cardinal's service, together with three sisters, were to be under the care of two priests.

An original idea, but, alas, never to be fulfilled in quite the ambitious way that Beaufort had intended. For whereas Beaufort had envisaged rich endowments, his own death and the Wars of the Roses upset his schemes so sadly that the Cardinal's successor to the throne of Winchester, the great William of Wayneflete, had little option but to reduce the permanent forces of the new foundation to two brethren and one chaplain.

Nevertheless, for all the trials and stresses of the times, the two foundations managed to continue side by side long after others had decayed and fallen into disuse, until today the Hospital of St Cross, with the Almshouse of Noble Poverty, can claim to be the oldest establishment of the kind in the country.

Today the two orders occupy the same buildings. There are twenty-seven brothers in all: eighteen under the original foundation and nine Beaufort brothers. Yet, though they are now as one, the two remain easily distinguishable. For while those of the older foundation wear black gowns and display the crutch cross of St John of Jerusalem, the Beaufort brothers wear claret-coloured gowns with the Cardinal's hat badge.

The poor without are no more forgotten than the poor within, the Wayfarer's Dole of a horn of beer and a slice of bread still being given to anyone who chooses to call at the Porter's Lodge around midday.

As might be expected of an institution so old, the brethren of St Cross are proud of their traditions. One of these traditions continues unto death. When a brother dies his silver cross is laid on a red velvet cushion and placed on his breast in his coffin; but before his burial this is removed again and fastened by the Master on to the gown of the new brother who is to succeed the deceased.

As St Cross is the oldest almshouse, so must its buildings rank among the most extensive and most beautiful of any such institution in the country. They cluster neatly round a well-kept square of grass and gravel paths. To the north is the Beaufort Tower with a niche containing a statue of the founder kneeling; and, next to it, the fine refectory, or Brethren's Hall, still with its central hearth where they used to burn their charcoal fires and the hole in the roof through which the smoke was to escape. To the west are the houses of the brothers, each containing two rooms and a pantry and opening on to a garden – a fascinating range that is rendered the more unusual by its strange series of chimneys. And opposite these houses, to the east, is the beautiful ambulatory, or cloister, leading to the north transept of the church of St Cross, itself a fine Norman building with many interesting features.

Chapter Eleven

SOME BUILDINGS WITH A STORY

WHILE the cathedral and the college naturally predominate in the old royal capital today, there are still many other buildings besides St Cross to be seen which have a place, either great or small, in the story of Winchester.

Castle Hall

Built on a hill, close by West Gate, Winchester's castle once commanded the entire town, enabling the king to protect the place against attack from outside and to ensure peace within. Though no less than thirty-five monarchs reigned at Winchester in their time, it was the Normans who built this great edifice. Probably one team of masons was at work upon the castle at the same time as another was engaged upon building the cathedral; for it was from here that William Rufus set off for his fateful hunting expedition in the New Forest.

Despite its position and appearance of might, the castle itself was totally destroyed in the Cromwellian troubles, leaving only the Great Hall standing. This hall and its predecessor appear to have been the most magnificent feature of the stronghold and the scene of many of Winchester's most colourful and historic events. Here were held the wedding receptions of Henry IV and Queen Mary, both of whom were married in the cathedral. Few scenes could have been more colourful than Bloody Mary's reception. She was adorned, we are told, with jewels of such brilliance that many who saw them lit up by the cathedral lights were momentarily blinded. As for her bridegroom, the unfortunate Philip of Spain, he wore cloth of gold and was supported by 4,000 attendants. After a service lasting from 11 a.m. until 3 p.m., all proceeded to the Great Hall, to the accompaniment of trumpets and bugles, there to partake of a dinner at which the Wykehamists recited Latin eulogies, and then dance into the night. Several of the medieval sovereigns were born in the castle, and one pretender to the throne, the Empress Matilda (daughter of Henry I), was forced to make an ignominious exit from the palace in a coffin during her struggles with King Stephen. Many of them held a reception in the hall after their coronation in the cathedral. Probably all held court here at some time or another.

When Edward I ascended the throne he held his first parliament in the Great Hall, basing it upon Earl Simon de Montfort's 'House of Commons'. Thereafter the hall became a recognized seat of parliament, and in one of the walls – the wall above the old dais – may still be seen a slit known as the King's Lug, provided to allow the king to listen to the deliberations of his Councillors without confusing the issue by appearing in person.

In this hall, too, Henry V was entertained by Cardinal Beaufort before setting sail to fight the Battle of Agincourt; while in later times Henry VIII received the Emperor Charles V here after his triumphant return from the Field of the Cloth of Gold.

The hall has seen grave times as well as gay. For it was here that Sir Walter Raleigh was sentenced to death after his farcical trial; here that Judge Jeffreys held his "Bloody Assizes' when on the Winchester circuit. The hall continued to be used for assize purposes until quite recent times. One of the principal exhibits is a round table bearing a portrait of King Arthur and the names of his knights. Though this is undoubtedly of great age, any suggestion that it may be the authentic 'Round Table' is clearly ridiculous.

West Gate

Of Winchester's various gates only two now remain: West Gate and King's Gate.

West Gate, near the Castle Hall, was built by Henry III and Richard II, and still bears evidence of the way it was designed to allow the defenders of the city to pour boiling lead on to the heads of the attackers.

Above the arch is a room that has been put to many uses in its time including that of a debtors' prison. Here, it seems, 'class distinction' was once much in evidence. If the debtor was a man of good birth he was reasonably well fed and allowed to pass his sentence in comparative comfort. Not so the common prisoner. He was accommodated in a hole under the floor, and when he grew hungry he was obliged to beg alms of passers-by or starve. To obtain his provisions he fixed a bag on to the end of a pole and then suspended this into the street, hoping that some kind-hearted person would take compassion upon him and drop something into the bag.

The old guard room of the West Gate now serves as one of the city museums and contains many interesting relics in the way of weights and measures, implements of punishment and the town's moot horn.

King's Gate

Though the origin of this gate is unknown it was probably built for the convenience of the Bishop, the Prior of St Swithun's and of the citizens generally, and mention of it is found as far back as 1148 in a survey of the city.

Above the arch is the little church of St Swithun, of great antiquarian interest. Though such churches were often built above gates during the Middle Ages, only very few have survived to the present day. It is thought that the church was originally intended as a chapel for the Priory servants, but quite early in its history it served as a parish church. Somewhere about 1263 it was burnt by the citizens following a dispute with the Prior. Whereupon three years later, in 1266, Prior Valentine entered into an agreement with the city authorities whereby the Priory undertook to maintain and fortify both King's Gate and South Gate and to open and close each upon the Mayor's command; in return for which undertaking the city acknowledged the gate as being the property of the Priory.

The building continued to serve as a parish church until 1925. Since then only one Sunday service each month has been conducted there, though many special services are arranged from time to time for weekdays. Rather heavily restored in the latter half of the seventeenth century, parts of its fabric are once again in need of attention; and in 1953 an appeal for £2,000 was made for this purpose.

Wolvesey Palace

In the Middle Ages and Tudor times Winchester had two castles: the one on the hill which, as we have seen, was used by the king, and the second, Wolvesey, at the bottom of the hill, which provided the chief seat of the bishops. Here, at Wolvesey, many of the bishops planned their reconstruction work on the cathedral; here, most likely, William of Wykeham conceived his plans for Winchester College. In this castle many a bishop entertained his sovereign. Bishop Gardiner entertained Queen Mary here on the eve of her wedding to Philip of Spain. The splendour of Wolvesey was second only to that of the sovereign's castle. . . . But then this building, too, was razed to the ground by the malicious Cromwell, leaving us only a few ruins.

Upon the Restoration, however, Charles II commissioned Sir Christopher Wren to build him a new and elaborate palace at Winchester – a scheme which, alas, was never completed – and Bishop Morley likewise arranged for the great architect to design a second palace of Wolvesey. Though the bishop's scheme, unlike the king's, was realized fully, the second Wolvesey was not to be left undisturbed either. Sadly neglected by Morley's successors, the greater part of it was pulled down in 1781, only a hundred years or so after its completion, by Bishop Brownlow North, who found it too costly to maintain. Only the west wing was left untouched, and this now serves as the home of the bishop.

City Cross

Standing some 43 feet high on a tier of steps, surmounted by a cross, and containing in its niches the figures of various bishops, including that of William of Wykeham, the City Cross – or Butter Cross as it is sometimes called – was erected by Cardinal Beaufort.

To this cross the farm folk of medieval and Tudor England traipsed on foot from the nearby villages to display their produce on the steps and then barter with one another, while the cross above stood as a symbol to remind them of the need to be honest in their dealings. As Winchester grew, and the number of shops multiplied, the City Cross ceased to serve its purpose; and in 1770 the city authorities agreed to sell it to an eccentric who was anxious to re-erect it in his private grounds as an ornament. Happily, however, the citizens of Winchester had more wisdom and more appreciation of their heritage than the city Fathers, for when the would-be purchaser arrived to take it away, Winchester turned out to a man to resist him. And so the old cross remains to this day as a proud link with the past.

The Deanery

A fifteenth-century stone building of great charm, the Deanery took its present form after the havoc caused by the Cromwellian soldiers had made a general remodelling of the Close necessary. While Queen Mary was given hospitality at Wolvesey on the eve of her wedding, her bridegroom, Philip, having arrived at Southampton from his native Spain in a rain storm, was accommodated at the Deanery for two nights. In later days, when the city was recovering from the disastrous rule of the Puritans, Charles II used to stay here while Sir Christopher Wren was building his palace. He came as the guest of Dean Meggot, an ugly little man by all accounts who gained the name of 'the bowing Dean' because of his complete subservience to his monarch. It is believed that Nell Gwynne sometimes accompanied the king on these visits and that a special room was built for her benefit. Force of circumstances made this necessary, it seems. In the first place Charles II had ordered Prebendary Ken (later Bishop Ken of Bath and Wells) to accommodate Nell in his house, but the high-principled Ken had no hesitation in flatly refusing to have anything to do with his sovereign's mistress. Whereupon the king turned to Meggot who once again bowed his acquiescence. Before long, however, Nell Gwynne was given her own house at the end of St Peter Street.

Adjoining the Deanery is the old Pilgrims' Cloister containing four pointed arches, one of which has been built into the house. Here the pilgrims to the shrine of St Swithun used to be given broken meat from the Prior's table before leaving.

Another interesting feature is a Roman pavement in the porch. This was transferred from the cathedral site.

Cheyney Court

Believed to take its name from the French word 'chene', meaning an oak, a massive tree having once stood in front of the building, this heavily timbered house with fourteenth- or fifteenth-century barge-boards and a fine range of stables, timber-framed with brick nogging, was once a place of considerable importance. Throughout the Middle Ages the bishops of Winchester enjoyed enormous power, and were rulers in their own right over a substantial area of the city. The district over which they ruled was known as the Soke from the Anglo-Saxon 'soc', meaning liberty. Cheyney Court served as the Soke's seat of government. Here dwelt the bishop's bailiff; and here were conducted the regular courts and 'burghmotes'. At regular intervals twelve of the most respected inhabitants of this district would be summoned to serve as a jury and sit in judgment over the many ruffians who were brought to Cheyney Court on charges of stealing eggs and other petty crimes. If they found a man guilty the bailiff might then recommend to the bishop that the culprit be put in the stocks or pillary and made a target at which to throw rotten eggs, that he be tied to the whipping-post, or else, perhaps, that he be shut up for a time in the dark, dank dungeons at Wolvesey.

The power of the court of Cheyney was supreme, and so it continued until 1835 when the municipal government of the city was reorganised.

God Begot House

This building in the High Street gains its strange name from the Latin, Domus Godbiete meaning a house granted to God. The original structure was given by Queen Emma, wife of Canute, to the monks of St Swithun's Priory together with a charter exempting it from all civil jurisdiction. As such it became a sanctuary house to which all offenders against the city's civic laws could flee in the sure knowledge that they would be given shelter. This purpose it continued to serve for more than five hundred years.

God Begot House was rebuilt in about 1550, and the front on to the street was completely remodelled in recent years. Though much of its character was thus destroyed, the upper story, approached by a side alley, retains its old charm and is still of great interest.

Chesil Rectory

This building served originally as the rectory of old St Peter's Church, and it takes its name from the street in which it is situated; a street originally called 'Chisil' meaning 'Strand'. Now used as a tea-rooms, it is a splendid half-timbered building, typical of those which lined the streets of Winchester in the fifteenth century.

City Bridge and Mill

The city's bridge and mill with the water leading away to the peaceful meadows provide a picturesque group close by Chesil Rectory. The mill was rebuilt of red brick in 1743 and extended four years later. In 1900 it ceased to be used for the grinding of corn, and later was bought by private subscription and presented to the National Trust. It is now leased to the Youth Hostels Association but is open to the public, free of charge, on Mondays, Tuesdays and Fridays.

The bridge, known as Soke Bridge from the days of the old Episcopal Soke when Cheyney Court provided a seat of government, was rebuilt of Portland stone in 1813. It spans the river with a single arch and contains a good balustraded parapet.

The Pentice

The modern shop can trace a clear evolution from the market cross. The earliest crosses consisted merely of a shaft rising from a series of steps upon which, as we have seen, the produce used to be displayed. When later it was decided to protect the produce against the weather and scavenging dogs it became customary to enclose the base of the cross. Then came the market hall with its series of arches for the display of goods; and from that, in turn, evolved the colonnaded range of open-fronted stalls, set back under a colonnade (formed by the overhanging upper storey, supported by pillars) along which the shoppers could walk in comfort while making their purchases.

Winchester's Pentice, close by the cross in High Street, affords a good example of this stage of the evolution. For, though naturally the shops themselves have been given modern fronts, the colonnade itself is of considerable age. Some of the buildings have barge-boards that are believed to be medieval, while many have beautiful bow windows and columns of later date.

26 & 27 Saint Swithun Street

While Sir Christopher Wren was in Winchester superintending the building of the new palace for Charles II he also designed a number of private houses, among them a house in St Swithun Street for the king's brother, James, Duke of York, later James II. Though many unfortunate alterations have since been made to the building, the house still bears several unmistakable Wren characteristics.

Jane Austen's House

After her health had been failing for a year, Jane Austen was brought to Winchester in May 1817 to be under the care of a local specialist. She was accommodated at No. 8 College Street, and there she died but two months later, on July 18th. She was buried, as has already been said, in the cathedral.

In Jane Austen's time the house was semi-detached in the style of the small town villa of the eighteenth century, but in 1953 the two houses were 'thrown into one' with a single front door, the whole front being thereby given a more well-to-do and more attractive air.

8 & 9 Kingsgate Street

During the reign of Charles II the king's favourite, the Duke of Buckingham, spent a great deal of time in Winchester, living in Kingsgate Street in a house which was then quite a large mansion.

Church of St Laurence

Not content with the great castle on the hill, William the Conqueror built himself a palace close by the spot where the city cross now stands. Badly damaged by fire in 1103, it was completely destroyed in the reign of Henry I. Since William's successors considered it unnecessary to rebuild the palace it was decided to erect a small church in the Perpendicular style in its stead: the church of St Laurence.

This church, which was rebuilt in the fifteenth century, has inherited not only the site of the palace but one of its customs. During the reign of the Conqueror every new Bishop of Winchester was required to call at the palace on his way to his enthronement as an act of loyalty to his sovereign. Upon the destruction of the palace it became customary for the bishops to call at the castle instead. During the last two hundred years or so, however, they have visited the church of St Laurence, there to change their shoes, ring a bell, pass a few moments in silent meditation and pay a fee to the rector.

But a few yards away, in The Square, is the old rectory of St Laurence. This small timbered building, recently restored, is now the 'Eclipse Inn'.

St John's Hospital

Founded, or possibly re-founded, in the latter part of the thirteenth century by John Devenish, an alderman of the city, St John's Hospital is one of the oldest almshouses in the country. The large medieval building which provides the living quarters was remodelled in the early years of George III's reign, but the church, with its row of typical lancet windows, is believed to have been left untouched.

Hyde Abbey

Founded by Edward the Elder as New Minster in fulfilment of a wish expressed in the will of his father, King Alfred, Hyde Abbey was first occupied in 1109. To this building were translated the bodies of Alfred and his queen, together with those of various Winchester bishops. For more than four centuries the abbey flourished, numbering among the most famous in the land. As its riches increased so its successive abbots spent more and more upon beautifying the buildings. Then came the dissolution of the monasteries and the decay of Hyde Abbey. Thus all that remain today are the stream that fed the abbey mill, the fifteenth-century gateway of the Abbot's lodging and a few odd fragments of masonry. On the site of the actual abbey stands an interesting building of the Restoration period, known as Hyde House.

City Museum

In a city with so long and rich a tradition as that of Winchester a visit to the local museum could hardly be otherwise than rewarding. Here, in the City Museum, are gathered together countless relics from countless ages. Material things that have survived long after buildings have perished, but which have played their part in the long story of Winchester: flint implements from the Stone Age; pottery fashioned by the Romans; ornaments and weapons recovered from the graves of the Anglo-Saxons; links with King Alfred; links with Jane Austen; links with every age and probably every reign.

But anyone who would wish to know Winchester will not be content to explore merely the historical. The buildings I have listed above are simply the more important. In the older part of the city – the original Winchester as opposed to that area which has developed in modern times in a way that is quite out of keeping with ancient tradition – nearly every street is a harbinger of graceful buildings: houses with imposing porches and fanlights, fascinating lintels or smooth bow windows. It is a town of nooks and crannies where the pilgrim feels impelled to walk to the end of the street to see what lies beyond the corner; a town which still rings the curfew at the close of day as it has done every day since William the Conqueror reigned here.

Chapter Twelve

AROUND WINCHESTER

WHILE Winchester has been an important centre of country
life for something like two thousand years, the focal point to
which men and women of many villages go to shop or worship,
she also provides an equally good centre from which to explore
the Hampshire countryside. Tucked away in the rolling
downland, or a little beyond, are many villages with interesting associations, historic buildings, or fascinating stories to
tell. Indeed, the stories of some are a part of the story of
Winchester herself.

The following are but a few of the nearby places that
merit a visit:

Avington

In this well-wooded corner of the valley of the River
Itchen stood the oak tree which Bishop Walkelin was careful
to preserve when collecting the timber for the foundation of
the cathedral, his reason for leaving this one tree untouched
being that it was believed that St Augustine had first
preached the Gospel there. Indeed, it has been suggested
that a gnarled and withering stump, still to be seen there,
may be the stump of that very tree though this seems highly
improbable.

Here, too, may be seen the red brick mansion where
Charles II stayed while Sir Christopher Wren was building
his new palace at Winchester.

Cheriton

This village is of interest as the scene of the great Battle of
Cheriton Down when the way was cleared for the final capture of Winchester by the Cromwellians during the Civil

War. It was said that close on two thousand troops were engaged in that battle and that nearly one thousand five hundred were killed; and at Lambly Lane are the burial mounds of the victims.

Basing

This enchanting village with its wealth of old cottages attractively grouped around the church was also the scene of an important Civil War battle. Here, in his stately Elizabethan mansion (built on the site of a Norman castle), the fifth Marquis of Winchester, staunch Royalist, held out heroically against the Cromwellians throughout a siege and many attacks extending over a period of close on two years. With a force of less than three hundred the marquis was able to repel attacks by more than seven thousand soldiers on horse and foot, eventually driving off Waller's men after many months of fighting. When the struggle was resumed with both sides reinforced, it took Waller a good eighteen months more before he was able to carry the house by assault. It is said that among the defenders were the architect, Inigo Jones, and the writer-divine, Thomas Fuller, who at one time served as chaplain to Hopton's men.

Though only the gatehouse and ruins of the great mansion remain, many links with the gallant Marquis of Winchester and his family may be found in the church.

Hursley

This village is also associated with the Commonwealth in that it was here that Richard Cromwell, Lord Protector of the Realm, spent many years after the Restoration, gaining considerable popularity locally as Squire 'Tumble-down-Dick', and devoting much of his time to playing bowls. Though Cromwell died in Hertfordshire at the age of eighty-six, he was buried in Hursley church; and there is a monument to the Cromwells under the tower.

Among Hursley's incumbents was John Keble who was vicar here for thirty years until his death in 1866. To Keble must go the chief credit for the foundation of the Oxford Movement; and it was to his memory that the Oxford college bearing his name was founded. At Hursley he was responsible for the introduction of much of the stained glass. He is buried in the churchyard, while inside the church he is also remembered by a cross in the floor of the chancel.

Selborne

This unspoilt corner of Hampshire has earned unusual fame in many lands as the home of another great divine, Gilbert White, whose grave in the churchyard bears the simple epigram: 'G. W. 26 June 1793.' He was born in the village and, like his grandfather before him, held the living at the time of his death. Indeed, he spent the greater part of his life in the village, living in a house (since much restored) called The Wakes, in whose garden a sundial which he erected remains to this day. It was, of course, as a naturalist and for his *Natural History of Selborne* that Gilbert White earned his fame; and the village is visited every year by hundreds of the famous vicar's admirers. As a centre for wild life it is still a happy hunting ground with many facets mentioned by Gilbert White yet to be seen.

Eversley

Rather less than thirty miles from Winchester are the church and rectory of Eversley where the celebrated author of *The Water Babies* and *Westward Ho!*, Charles Kingsley, ministered for thirty-three years until his death in 1875. Here, to the south side of the church, may be found the grave of Kingsley and his wife: a grave with a Maltese cross bearing the simple words, 'God is Love'.

Upon Kingsley's death a sum of £1,200 was raised in order to carry out various restorations in his memory.

Steventon

Of all the great writers of the past none is more closely associated with Hampshire than Jane Austen, who, as we have seen, died at Winchester and is buried in the cathedral. It was at Steventon – where her father, the Rev. George Austen, was rector for over forty years – that she was born From earliest childhood she revealed an aptitude for writing stories, and while still at Steventon, before she was twenty-two, she wrote two of her most famous books, *Sense and Sensibility* and *Pride and Prejudice*, though these were not published until many years later.

Though, unfortunately, the rectory where Jane Austen was born has since been destroyed, the church where she listened every Sunday to her father's sermons is but little altered.

Chawton

After her father's death in 1805 Jane Austen and her family, having already left Steventon for Bath, moved first to Southampton and thence, four years later, to Chawton. Here she spent the last years of her life before being sent to Winchester to be under the care of a specialist; and here she wrote at least two more of the books that were to earn her lasting fame, *Emma* and *Mansfield Park*, though none of her works were published under her own name until the year after her death when *Northanger Abbey* and *Persuasion* were issued. Chawton House, a sixteenth-century building with later additions, where Jane Austen spent those eight productive years, is in the centre of the village and is open to the public at certain stipulated times.

Romsey

This old country town has a close affinity with Winchester in that its famous abbey, like New Minster and Nunnaminster at Winchester, is also believed to have been founded by Edward the Elder in accordance with the wishes of his father, Alfred the Great. Moreover, it seems probable that the present abbey church was built by Winchester's celebrated bishop, Henry de Blois.

Among the many interesting buildings to be seen in the town, besides the abbey, is the hunting lodge which King John built for himself in 1206. This house has played many parts in its time. After John's death it was presented to the abbey as a guest house; but after the dissolution of the monasteries it became a private residence and later a workhouse.

On the edge of the town, standing in spacious grounds, is Broadlands, the former home of Lord Palmerston, where Florence Nightingale often consulted the Prime Minister before setting off on her nursing mission to the Crimea. Here the Queen, as Princess Elizabeth, and the Duke of Edinburgh spent the first few days of their honeymoon.

Tichborne

This village, charming in itself, is the scene of an unusual custom when, on Lady Day, the Tichborne Dole is distributed by the lord of the manor. Before an enormous bin of flour, set up in front of the great house of the Tichbornes, the parson conducts a service at which the soul of Lady Mabella de Tichborne, who lived at the time of Henry I, is prayed for. At the end of that service the flour is sprinkled with Holy Water and blessed, and is then distributed at the rate of a gallon to every man and half a gallon to every woman and child by the holder of the Tichborne title. The flour is made from wheat grown on an area of the estate known as The Crawls, and this name, like the custom itself, is derived from the fact that when Lady Mabella was dying she implored her husband to set aside an area of land upon which to grow food for the poor – only to be handed a candle by the hard-hearted Sir Roger de Tichborne with the promise that he would devote just so much of his estate to this purpose as she was able to circumvent before the flame was extinguished. Being so weak, she was unable to do more than crawl; yet she managed to cover as much as twenty-three acres.

Hambledon

This village, on the edge of Broadhalfpenny Down, with its quaint little 'Bat and Ball Inn', is renowned as having been the headquarters of cricket before the days of Lord's. Here, on the down, the players played in breeches and cocked or top hats, using only two stumps, bowling under-arm, and wielding a bat not unlike a rather cumbersome hockey stick. Many of the matches were played for stakes as high as £500, and many of the leading statesmen in the land used to drive to Hambledon to play or watch. Lord Palmerston's father paid many visits from Broadlands. Though considerably altered since the days when the players met there to drink prodigious quantities of port, the inn has an interesting gallery of cricketing photographs from those times.

Besides the many villages to explore, Winchester affords a convenient gateway, via Romsey, to the New Forest. This forest, with its wealth of oaks, beeches, holly and yew has a deep niche in the story of Winchester; for it was preserved as the hunting ground of William the Conqueror and his privileged followers. Here were sown the seeds of the Game Laws in all their harshness: laws that condemned a man to have his eyes plucked out or his feet chopped off for the most trivial offences. Could it have been on account of his harshness in enforcing those laws that William Rufus met his death so unluckily in this forest? Only Sir Walter Tyrrell could have supplied that answer, but they say that once a year the water in the pond near Canterton Glen where he washed his hands after shooting the fatal arrow still turns red as if to prove that his hands were blood-stained.

INDEX